Granv
Prefaces t

—

MACBETH

Foreword by
Richard Eyre

NT
NATIONAL

N
H
B

NICK HERN BOOKS

First published in this collected paperback edition in 1993 jointly by
Nick Hern Books Limited, 14 Larden Road, London W3 7ST
and the Royal National Theatre, London,
by arrangement with Batsford.

Preface to Macbeth. Originally published in 1923, revised 1930

Set in 10/11 Baskerville by Pure Tech Corporation, Pondicherry
(India)
Printed in Australia by
Australian Print Group

A CIP catalogue record for this book is available from the British
Library

ISBN 1 85459 167 3

Shakespeare Alive!

The history of the theatre in England in this century can be told largely through the lives and work of two men: George Bernard Shaw and Harley Granville Barker, a triple-barrelled cadence of names that resonates like the ruffling of the pages of a large book in a silent public library. One was a brilliant polemicist who dealt with certainties and assertions and sometimes, but not often enough, breathed life into his sermons; the other a committed sceptic who started from the premise that the only thing certain about human behaviour was that nothing was certain. Both, however, possessed a passionate certainty about the importance of the theatre and the need to revise its form, its content, and the way that it was managed. Shaw was a playwright, critic and pamphleteer, Barker a playwright, director and actor.

The Voysey Inheritance is, at least in my opinion, Granville Barker's best play: a complex web of family relationships, a fervent but never unambiguous indictment of a world dominated by the mutually dependent obsessions of greed, class, and self-deception. It's also a virtuoso display of stagecraft: the writer showing that as director he can handle twelve speaking characters on stage at one time, and that as actor he can deal with the most ambitious and unexpected modulations of thought and feeling. The 'inheritance' of the Voyseys is a legacy of debt, bad faith, and bitter family dissension. Edward's father has, shortly before his death, revealed that he has been cheating the family firm of solicitors for many years, as his father had for many years before that. Towards the end of the play Edward Voysey, the youngest son, confronts the woman he loves:

> EDWARD. Why wouldn't he own the truth to me about himself?
>
> BEATRICE. Perhaps he took care not to know it. Would you have understood?
>
> EDWARD. Perhaps not. But I loved him.
>
> BEATRICE. That would silence a bench of judges.

Shaw would have used the story to moralise and polemicise. He might have had the son hate the father; he might have had him forgive him; he might have had him indict him as a paradigm of capitalism; he would never have said he loved him.

Everybody needs a father, or, failing that, a father-figure. He may be a teacher, a prophet, a boss, a priest perhaps, a political leader, a friend, or, sometimes, if you are very lucky, the real one. If you can't find a father you must invent him. In some ways, not altogether trivial, Granville Barker is something of a father-figure for me. He's a writer whom I admire more than any twentieth-century English writer before the sixties – Chekhov with an English accent; he's the first modern British director; he's the real founder of the National Theatre and, in his *Prefaces*, he's a man who, alone amongst Shakespearean commentators before Jan Kott, believed in the power of Shakespeare on stage.

There was a myth that Granville Barker was the natural son of Shaw. He was certainly someone whom Shaw could, in his awkward way, cherish and admire, educate and castigate. When Barker fell wildly in love ('in the Italian manner' as Shaw said) with Helen Huntington, an American millionairess, he married her, acquired a hyphen in his surname, moved first to Devon to play the part of a country squire, and then to France to a life of seclusion. Shaw thought that he had buried himself alive and could never reconcile himself to the loss. It was, as his biographer

Hesketh Pearson said: 'The only important matter about which he asked me to be reticent.'

After directing many of Shaw's plays for many years, acting many of his best roles (written by Shaw with Barker in mind), dreaming and planning together the birth of a National Theatre, not to mention writing, directing, and acting in his own plays while managing his own company at the Royal Court, Barker withdrew from the theatre, and for twenty years there was silence between the two men. Only on the occasion of the death of Shaw's wife did they communicate by letters. 'I did not know I could be so moved by anything,' wrote Shaw to him.

Out of this self-exile came one major work, slowly assembled over many years: *The Prefaces to Shakespeare*. With a few exceptions (Auden on *Othello*, Barbara Everett on *Hamlet*, Jan Kott on *The Tempest*) it's the only critical work about Shakespeare that's made any impact on me, apart, that is, from my father's view of Shakespeare, which was brief and brutal: 'It's absolute balls.'

As much as we need a good father, we need a good teacher. Mine, improbably perhaps, was Kingsley Amis. He'd arrived, somewhat diffidently, at Cambridge at the same time as I did. The depth of my ignorance of English literature corresponded almost exactly to his dislike of the theatre. Nevertheless, he made me see Shakespeare with a mind uncontaminated by the views of academics, whom he would never have described as his fellows and whose views he regarded as, well, academic. I would write essays marinated in the opinions of Spurgeon, Wilson Knight, Dover Wilson and a large cast of critical supernumeraries. He would gently, but courteously, cast aside my essay about, say, *Twelfth Night*: 'But what do *you* think of this play? Do you think it's any good?' 'Well . . . er . . . it's Shakespeare.' 'Yes, but is it any *good*? I mean as a *play*. It says it's a comedy. Fine. But does it have any decent jokes?'

I took this for irreverence, heresy even. Over the years, however, I've come to regard this as good teaching, or, closely allied, good direction. It's asking the right questions, unintimidated by reputation, by tradition, by received opinion, or by critical orthodoxy. This was shocking, but healthy, for a young and impressionable man ripe to become a fundamentalist in matters of literary taste and ready to revere F. R. Leavis as the Ayatollah of 'Cambridge English'. What you have is yourself and the text, only that. That's the lesson of Granville Barker: 'We have the text to guide us, half a dozen stage directions, and that is all. I abide by the text and the demands of the text and beyond that I claim freedom.' I can't imagine a more useful and more enduring dictum.

The Prefaces have a practical aim: 'I want to see Shakespeare made fully effective on the English stage. That is the best sort of help I can lend.' What Granville Barker wrote is a primer for directors and actors working on the plays of Shakespeare. There is lamentably little useful literature about the making of theatre, even though there is an indigestible glut of memoirs and biographies, largely concerned with events that have taken place *after* the curtain has fallen. If I was asked by a visiting Martian to recommend books which would help him, her or it to make theatre in the manner of the European I could only offer four books: Stanislavsky on *The Art of the Stage*, John Willett's *Brecht on Theatre*, Peter Brook's *The Empty Space*, and *The Prefaces to Shakespeare*.

Stanislavsky offers a pseudo-scientific dissection of the art of acting which is, in some respects, like reading Freud on the mechanism of the joke: earnest, well-meaning, but devoid of the indispensable ingredient of its subject matter: humour. Stanislavsky's great contribution was to demand that actors hold the mirror up to nature, that they take their craft as seriously as the writers they served, and to provide some sort of formal discipline within which both aims could be realised.

Brecht provided a manifesto that was a political and aesthetic response to the baroque encrustations of the scenery-laden, star-dominated, archaic boulevard theatre of Germany in the twenties. Although much of what he wrote as theory is an unpalatable mix of political ideology and artistic instruction, it is his theatrical instinct that prevails. He asserts, he insists, he browbeats. He demands that the stage, like society, must be re-examined, reformed, that the audience's habits mustn't be satisfied, they must be changed, but just when he is about to nail his 13 Articles to the church door he drops the voice of the zealot: 'The stage is not a hothouse or a zoological museum full of stuffed animals. It must be peopled with live, three-dimensional self-contradictory people with their passions, unconsidered utterances and actions.' In all art forms, he says, the guardians of orthodoxy will assert that there are eternal and immutable laws that you ignore at your peril, but in the theatre there is only one inflexible rule: 'The proof of the pudding is in the eating.' Brecht teaches us to ask the question: what goes on in a theatre?

Brook takes that question even further: what *is* theatre? It's a philosophical, but eminently practical, question that Brook has been asking for over 30 years and which has taken him to the African desert, a quarry in Iran, and an abandoned music hall in Paris. 'I take an empty space and call it a bare stage. A man walks across this empty space while someone else is watching him, and that is all that is needed for an act of theatre to be engaged.' For all his apparent concern with metaphyics, there is no more practical man of the theatre than Brook.

I was once at a seminar where someone asked him what was the job of the director. 'To get the actors on and off stage,' he said. Like Brecht, like Stanislavsky, like Granville Barker, Brook argues that for the theatre to be expressive it must be, above all, simple and unaffected: a distillation of language, of gesture, of action, of design, where meaning is the essence. The meaning must be felt as much as understood. 'They don't have to understand with their ears,' says Granville Barker, 'just with their guts.'

Brecht did not acknowledge a debt to Granville Barker. Perhaps he was not aware of one, but it seems to me that Barker's Shakespeare productions were the direct antecedents of Brecht's work. He certainly knew enough about English theatre to know that he was on to a good thing adapting *The Beggar's Opera, The Recruiting Officer* and *Coriolanus*. Brecht has been lauded for destroying illusionism; Granville Barker has been unhymned. He aimed at re-establishing the relationship between actor and audience that had existed in Shakespeare's theatre – and this at a time when the prevailing style of Shakespearean production involved *not* stopping short of having live sheep in *As You Like It*. He abolished footlights and the proscenium arch, building out an apron over the orchestra pit which Shaw said 'apparently trebled the spaciousness of the stage. . . . To the imagination it looks as if he had invented a new heaven and a new earth.'

His response to staging Shakespeare was not to look for a synthetic Elizabethanism. 'We shall not save our souls by being Elizabethan.' To recreate the Globe would, he knew, be aesthetic anasthaesia, involving the audience in an insincere conspiracy to pretend that they were willing collaborators in a vain effort to turn the clock back. His answers to staging Shakespeare were similar to Brecht's for *his* plays and, in some senses, to

Chekhov's for his. He wanted scenery not to decorate and be literal, but to be expressive and metaphorical, and at the same time, in apparent contradiction, to be specific and be real, while being minimal and iconographic: the cart in *Mother Courage*, the nursery in *The Cherry Orchard*, the dining table in *The Voysey Inheritance*. 'To create a new hieroglyphic language of scenery. That, in a phrase, is the problem. If the designer finds himself competing with the actors, the sole interpreters Shakespeare has licensed, then it is he that is the intruder and must retire.'

In *The Prefaces* Granville Barker argues for a fluency of staging unbroken by scene changes. Likewise the verse should be spoken fast. 'Be swift, be swift, be not poetical,' he wrote on the dressing-room mirror of Cathleen Nesbitt when she played Perdita. Within the speed, however, detailed reality. *Meaning* above all.

It is the director's task, with the actors, to illuminate the meanings of a play: its vocabulary, its syntax, and its philosophy. The director has to ask what each scene is revealing about the characters and their actions: what story is each scene telling us? In *The Prefaces* Granville Barker exhumes, examines and explains the lost stagecraft of Shakespeare line by line, scene by scene, play by play.

Directing Shakespeare is a matter of understanding the meaning of a scene and staging it in the light of that knowledge. Easier said than done, but it's at the heart of the business of directing any play, and directing Shakespeare is merely directing writ large. Beyond that, as David Mamet has observed, 'choice of actions and adverbs constitute the craft of directing'. Get up from that chair and walk across the room. Slowly.

With Shakespeare as with any other playwright the director's job is to make the play live, now, in the present tense. 'Spontaneous enjoyment is the life of the theatre,' says Granville Barker in his Preface to *Love's Labour's Lost*. To receive a review, as Granville Barker did, headed *SHAKESPEARE ALIVE!* is the most, but should be the least, that a director must hope for.

I regard Granville Barker not only as the first modern English director but as the most influential. Curiously, partly as a result of his early withdrawal from the theatre, partly because his *Prefaces* have been out of print for many years, and partly because of his own self-effacement, he has been unjustly ignored both in the theatre and in the academic world, where the codification of their 'systems' has resulted in the canonisation of Brecht and Stanislavsky. I hope the re-publication of *The Prefaces* will right the balance. Granville Barker himself always thought of them as his permanent legacy to the theatre.

My sense of filial identification is not entirely a professional one. When I directed *The Voysey Inheritance* I wanted a photograph of the author on the poster. A number of people protested that it was the height, or depth, of vanity and self-aggrandisement to put my own photograph on the poster. I was astonished, I was bewildered, but I was not unflattered. I still can't see the resemblance, but it's not through lack of trying.

Two years ago the Royal National Theatre was presented with a wonderful bronze bust of Granville Barker by Katherine Scott (the wife, incidentally, of the Antarctic hero). For a while it sat on the windowsill of my office like a benign household god. Then it was installed on a bracket in the foyer opposite a bust of Olivier, the two men eyeing each other in wary mutual regard. A few months later it was stolen; an act of homage perhaps. I miss him.

Richard Eyre

Introduction

We have still much to learn about Shakespeare the playwright. Strange that it should be so, after three centuries of commentary and performance, but explicable. For the Procrustean methods of a changed theatre deformed the plays, and put the art of them to confusion; and scholars, with this much excuse, have been apt to divorce their Shakespeare from the theatre altogether, to think him a poet whose use of the stage was quite incidental, whose glory had small relation to it, for whose lapses it was to blame.

The Study and the Stage

THIS much is to be said for Garrick and his predecessors and successors in the practice of reshaping Shakespeare's work to the theatre of their time. The essence of it was living drama to them, and they meant to keep it alive for their public. They wanted to avoid whatever would provoke question and so check that spontaneity of response upon which acted drama depends. Garrick saw the plays, with their lack of 'art', through the spectacles of contemporary culture; and the bare Elizabethan stage, if it met his mind's eye at all, doubtless as a barbarous makeshift. Shakespeare was for him a problem; he tackled it, from our point of view, misguidedly and with an overplus of enthusiasm. His was a positive world; too near in time, moreover, as well as too opposed in taste to Shakespeare's to treat it perspectively. The romantic movement might have brought a more concordant outlook. But by then the scholars were off their own way; while the theatre began to think of its Shakespeare from the point of view of the picturesque, and, later, in terms of upholstery. Nineteenth-century drama developed along the lines of realistic illusion, and the staging of Shakespeare was further subdued to this, with inevitably disastrous effect on the speaking of his verse; there was less perversion of text perhaps, but actually more wrenching of the construction of the plays for the convenience of the stage carpenter. The public appetite for this sort of thing having been gorged, producers then turned to newer—and older—contrivances, leaving 'realism' (so called) to the modern comedy that had fathered it. Amid much vaporous theorizing—but let us humbly own how hard it is not to write nonsense about art, which seems ever pleading to be enjoyed and not written about at all—the surprising discovery had been made that varieties of stagecraft and stage were not historical accidents but artistic obligations, that Greek drama belonged in a Greek theatre, that Elizabethan plays, therefore, would, presumably, do best upon an Elizabethan stage, that there was nothing sacrosanct about scenery, footlights, drop-curtain or any of their belongings. This brings us to the present situation.

There are few enough Greek theatres in which Greek tragedy can be played; few enough people want to see it, and they will applaud it encouragingly however it is done. Some acknowledgement is due to the altruism of the doers! Shakespeare is another matter. The English theatre, doubtful of its destiny, of necessity venal, opening its doors to all comers, seems yet, as by some instinct, to seek renewal of strength in him. An actor, unless success has made him cynical, or his talent be merely trivial, may take some pride in the hall mark of Shakespearean achievement. So may a manager if he thinks he can afford it. The public (or their spokesmen) seem to consider Shakespeare and his genius a sort of national property, which, truly, they do nothing to conserve, but in which they have moral rights not lightly to be flouted. The production of the plays is thus still apt to be marked by a timid respect for 'the usual thing'; their acting is crippled by pseudo-traditions, which are inert because they are not Shakespearean at all. They are the accumulation of two centuries of progressive misconception and distortion of his playwright's art. On the other hand, England has been spared production of Shakespeare according to this or that even more irrelevant theory of presentationalism, symbolism, constructivism or what not. There is the breach in the wall of 'realism', but we have not yet made up our minds to pass through, taking our Shakespeare with us.

Incidentally, we owe the beginning of the breach to Mr William Poel, who, with fanatical courage, when 'realism' was at the tottering height of its triumph in the later revivals of Sir Henry Irving, and the yet more richly upholstered revelations of Sir Herbert Tree, thrust the Elizabethan stage in all its apparent eccentricity upon our unwilling notice.¹ Mr Poel shook complacency. He could not expect to do much more; for he was a logical reformer. He showed us the Elizabethan stage, with Antony and Cleopatra, Troilus and Cressida, in their ruffs and farthingales as for Shakespeare's audiences they lived. Q.E.D. There, however, as far as the popular theatre was concerned, the matter seemed to rest for twenty years or so. But it was just such a demonstration that was needed; anything less drastic and provocative might have been passed over with mild approval.

To get the balance true, let us admit that while Shakespeare was an Elizabethan playwright he was—and now is to us—predominantly something much more. Therefore we had better not too unquestioningly thrust him back within the confines his genius has escaped, nor presume him to have felt the pettier circumstances of his theatre sacrosanct. Nor can we turn Elizabethans as we watch the plays; and every mental effort to do so will subtract from our enjoyment of them. This is the case against the circumstantial reproduction of Shakespeare's staging. But Mr Poel's achievement remains; he cleared for us from Shakespeare's stagecraft the scenic rubbish by which it had been so long encumbered and disguised. And we could now, if we would, make a promising fresh start. For the scholars, on their side, have lately—the scholarly among them—cut clear of the transcendental fog (scenic illusion of another sort) in which their nineteenth-century peers loved to lose themselves, and they too are beginning again at the beginning. A text acquires virtue now by its claim to be a prompt book, and the most comprehensive work of our time upon the Elizabethan stage is an elaborate sorting-out of plays, companies and theatres. On Dr Pollard's treatment of the texts and on the foundations of fact laid by Sir Edmund Chambers a new scholarship is rising, aiming first to see Shakespeare in the theatre for which he wrote. It is a scholarship, therefore, by which the theatre of today can profit, to which, by its acting of Shakespeare, it could contribute, one would hope. Nor should the scholars disdain the help; for criticism cannot live upon criticism, it needs refreshment from the living art. Besides, what is all the criticism and scholarship finally for if not to keep Shakespeare alive? And he must always be most alive—even if roughly and rudely alive—in the theatre. Let the scholars force a way in there, if need be. Its fervid atmosphere will do them good; the benefit will be mutual.

These Prefaces are an attempt to profit by this new scholarship and to contribute to it some research into Shakespeare's stagecraft, by examining the plays, one after another, in the light of the interpretation he designed for them, so far as this can be deduced; to discover, if possible, the production he would have desired for them, all merely incidental circumstances apart. They might profit more written a generation hence, for the ground they build upon is still far from clear. And this introduction is by no means a conspectus of the subject; that can only come as a sequel. There has been, in this branch of Shakespearean study, too much generalization and far too little analysis of material.[2]

Shakespeare's Stagecraft

SHAKESPEARE'S own career was not a long one. The whole history of the theatre he wrote for does not cover a century. Between Marlowe and Massinger, from the first blaze to the glowing of the embers, it is but fifty years. Yet even while Shakespeare was at work, the stage to which he fitted his plays underwent constant and perhaps radical change. From Burbage's first theatre to the Globe, then to Blackfriars, not to mention excursions to Court and into the great halls—change of audiences and their behaviour, of their taste, development of the art of acting, change of the stage itself and its resources were all involved in the progress, and are all, we may be sure, reflected to some degree in the plays themselves. We guess at the conditions of each sort of stage and theatre, but there is often the teasing question to which of them had a play, as we have it now, been adapted. And of the 'private' theatre, most in vogue for the ten years preceding the printing of the First Folio so far we know least. The dating of texts and their ascription to the usages of a particular theatre may often be a searchlight upon their stagecraft. Here is much work for the new scholarship.

Conversely, the watchful working-out of the plays in action upon this stage or that would be of use to the scholars, who otherwise must reconstruct their theatre and gloss their texts as in a vacuum. The play was once fitted to the stage; it is by no means impossible to rebuild that stage now, with its doors, balconies, curtains and machines, by measuring the needs of the play. It is idle, for instance, to imagine scenes upon inner or upper stage without evidence that they will be audible or visible there; and editing is still vitiated by lack of this simple knowledge. Here, if nowhere else, this present research must fall short, for its method should rightly be experimental; more than one mind should be at work on it, moreover.

The text of a play is a score waiting performance, and the performance and its preparation are, almost from the beginning, a work of collaboration. A producer may direct the preparation, certainly. But if he only knows how to give orders, he has mistaken his vocation; he had better be a drill-sergeant. He might talk to his company when they all met together for the first time to study *Love's Labour's Lost, Julius Cæsar* or *King Lear*, on some such lines as these Prefaces pursue, giving a considered opinion of the play, drawing a picture of it in action, providing, in fact, a hypothesis which mutual study would prove—and might partly disprove. No sort of study of a play can better the preparation of its performance if this is rightly done. The matured art of the playwright lies in giving life to characters in action, and the secret of it in giving each character a due chance in the battle, the action of a play becoming literally the fighting of a battle of character. So the greater the playwright, the wider and deeper his sympathies, the more genuine this opposition will be and the less easily will a single mind grasp it, as it must be grasped, in the fullness of its emotion. The dialogue of a play runs—and often intricately—upon lines of reason, but it is charged besides with an emotion which speech releases, yet only releases fully when the speaker is—as an actor is—identified with the character. There is further the incidental action, implicit in the dialogue, which springs to life only when a scene is in being. A play, in fact, as we find it written, is a magic spell; and even the magician cannot always foresee the full effect of it.

Not every play, it must be owned, will respond to such intensive study. Many, ambitiously conceived, would collapse under the strain. Many are mere occasions for display of their actors' wit or eloquence, good looks or nice behaviour, and meant to be no more; and if they are skilfully contrived the parts fit together and the whole machine should go like clockwork. Nor, in fact, are even the greatest plays often so studied. There is hardly a theatre in the world where masterpiece and trumpery alike are not rushed through rehearsals to an arbitrarily effective performance, little more learned of them than the words, gaps in the understanding of them filled up with 'business'—effect without cause, the demand for this being the curse of the theatre as of other arts, as of other things than art. Not to such treatment will the greater plays of Shakespeare yield their secrets. But working upon a stage which reproduced the essential conditions of his, working as students, not as showmen merely, a company of actors might well find many of the riddles of the library answering themselves unasked. And these Prefaces could best be a record of such work, if such work were to be done.

We cannot, on the other hand, begin our research by postulating the principles of the Elizabethan stage. One is tempted to say it had none, was too much a child of nature to bother about such things. Principles were doubtless imposed upon it when it reached respectability, and heads would be bowed to the yoke. Shakespeare's among them? He had served a most practical apprenticeship to his trade. If he did not hold horses at the door, he sat behind the curtains, we may be sure, and held the prompt book on occasion. He acted, he cobbled other men's plays, he could write his own to order. Such a one may stay a journeyman if he is not a genius, but he will not become a doctrinaire. Shakespeare's work shows such principles as the growth of a tree shows. It is not haphazard merely because it is not formal; it is shaped by inner strength. The theatre, as he found it, allowed him and encouraged him to great freedom of development. Because the material resources of a stage are simple, it does not follow that the technique of its playwriting will stay so. Crude work may show up more crudely, when there are none of the fal-lals of illusion to disguise it that the modern theatre provides. But, if he has it in him, a dramatist can, so unfettered, develop the essentials of his art more boldly and more subtly too. The Elizabethan drama made an amazingly quick advance from crudity to an excellence which was often technically most elaborate. The advance and the not less amazing gulf which divides its best from its worst may be ascribed to the simplicity of the machinery it employed. That its decadence was precipitated by the influence of the Masque and the shifting of its centre of interest from the barer public stage to the candle-lit private theatre, where the machinery of the Masque became effective, it would be rash to assert; but the occurrences are suspiciously related. Man and machine (here at any rate is a postulate, if a platitude!) are false allies in the theatre, secretly at odds; and when man gets the worst of it, drama is impoverished; and the struggle, we may add, is perennial. No great drama depends upon pageantry. All great drama tends to concentrate upon character; and, even so, not upon picturing men as they show themselves to the world like figures on a stage—though that is how it must ostensibly show them—but on the hidden man. And the progress of Shakespeare's art from *Love's Labour's Lost* to *Hamlet*, and thereafter with a difference, lies in the simplifying of this paradox and the solving of the problem it presents; and the process involves the developing of a very subtle sort of stagecraft indeed.

For one result we have what we may call a very self-contained drama. Its chief values, as we know, have not changed with the fashions of the theatre. It relies much on the music of the spoken word, and a company of schoolchildren with pleasant voices, and an ear for rhythm, may vociferate through a play to some effect. It is as much to be enjoyed in the reading, if we hear it in imagination as we read, as drama meant to be acted can be. As with its simplicities then, so it should be, we presume, with its complexities. The subtly emotional use of verse and the interplay of motive and character, can these not be appreciated apart from the bare boards of their original setting? It does not follow. It neither follows that the advantages of the Elizabethan stage were wholly negative nor that, with our present knowledge, we can imagine the full effect of a play in action upon it. The imagining of a play in action is, under no circumstances, an easy thing.[3] What would one not give to go backward through the centuries to see the first performance of *Hamlet*, played as Shakespeare had it played![4] In default, if we could but make ourselves read it as if it were a manuscript fresh from its author's hands! There is much to be said for turning one's back on the editors, even, when possible, upon the First Folio with its demarcation of acts and scenes, in favour of the Quartos—Dr Pollard's 'good' Quartos—in their yet greater simplicity.

The Convention of Place

IT is, for instance, hard to discount the impression made merely by reading: *Scene i—Elsinore. A platform before the Castle*; and most of us have, to boot, early memories of painted battlements and tenth-century castles (of ageing Hamlets and their portly mothers for that matter) very difficult to dismiss. No great harm, one protests; it was a help, perhaps, to the unimaginative. But it is a first step to the certain misunderstanding of Shakespeare's stagecraft. The 'if, how and when' of the presenting of localities on the Elizabethan stage is, of course, a complex question. Shakespeare himself seems to have followed, consciously, no principles in the matter, nor was his practice very logical, nor at all consistent. It may vary with the play he is writing and the particular stage he is writing for; it will best be studied in relation to each play. We can, however, free ourselves from one general misconception which belongs to our own over-logical standpoint. When we learn with a shock of surprise—having begun in the schoolroom upon the Shakespeare of the editors, it comes as belated news to us—that neither battlements, throne rooms nor picturesque churchyards were to be seen at the Globe, and that *Elsinore. A platform before the Castle* is not Shakespeare at all, we yet imagine ourselves among the audience there busily conjuring these things up before the eye of faith. The Elizabethan audience was at no such pains. Nor was this their alternative to seeing the actors undisguisedly concerned with the doors, curtains and balconies which, by the play's requirements, should have been anything but what they were. As we, when a play has no hold on us, may fall to thinking about the scenery, so to a Globe audience, unmoved, the stage might be an obvious bare stage. But are we conscious of the scenery behind the actor when the play really moves us? If we are, there is something very wrong with the scenery, which should know its place as a background. The audience was not conscious of curtain and balcony when Burbage played Hamlet to them. They were conscious of Hamlet. That conventional background faded as does our painted illusion, and they certainly did not deliberately conjure up in its place mental pictures of Elsinore. The genus audience is passive, if expectant, imaginatively lazy till roused, never, one may be sure, at pains to make any effort that is generally unnecessary to enjoyment.

With Shakespeare the locality of a scene has dramatic importance, or it has none; and this is as true of his early plays as his late ones. Both in *Richard II* and *Antony and Cleopatra*, scene after scene passes with no exact indication of where we may be. With *Cleopatra* we are surely in Egypt, with Cæsar in Rome. Pompey appears, and the talk tells us that both Egypt and Rome are elsewhere; but positively where Pompey is at the moment we never learn.[5] Indoors or outdoors? The action of the scene or the clothing of the characters will tell us this if we need to know. But, suddenly transported to the Parthian war, our whereabouts is made amply plain. It is, however, made plain by allusion. The information peeps out through talk of kindred things; we are hardly aware we are being told, and, again, we learn no more than we need to learn. This, truly, is a striking development from the plump and plain

> Barkloughly Castle call they this at hand?

of Richard II, even from the more descriptive

> I am a stranger here in Gloucestershire:
> These high wild hills and rough, uneven ways
> Draw out our miles. . .

by which Shakespeare pictures and localizes the manoeuvres of Richard and Bolingbroke when he wants to.
But the purpose is the same, and the method essentially
the same.[6] Towards the end of the later play come scene
after scene of the marching and countermarching of
armies, of fighting, of truce, all the happenings of three
days' battle. Acts III and IV contain twenty-eight scenes
long and short; some of them are very short; three of
them have but four lines apiece. The editors conscien-
tiously ticket them *A plain near Actium, Another part of the
plain, Another part of the plain* and so on, and conclude
that Shakespeare is really going too far and too fast, is indeed
(I quote Sir Edmund Chambers) 'in some danger of
outrunning the apprehensions of his auditory.' Indeed he
might be if this cinematographic view of his intentions
were the right one! But it utterly falsifies them. Show an
audience such a succession of painted scenes—if you
could at the pace required—and they would give attention to nothing else whatever; the drama would pass
unnoticed. Had Shakespeare tried to define the whereabouts of every scene in any but the baldest phrases—the
protesting editors seem not to see that he makes no
attempt to; only *they* do!—he would have had to lengthen
and complicate them; had he written only a labelling
line or two he would still have distracted his audience
from the essential drama. Ignoring whereabouts, letting
it at most transpire when it naturally will, the characters
capture all attention. This is the true gain of the bare
stage; unless to some dramatic end no precious words
need be spent, in complying with the undramatic demands of space and time; incarnation of character can
be all in all. Given such a crisis as this the gain is yet
greater. We are carried through the phases of the three
days' battle; and what other stage convention would
allow us so varied a view of it, could so isolate the true

drama of it? For do we not pass through such a crisis in reality with just that indifference to time and place? These scenes, in their kind, show Shakespeare's stage-craft, not at its most reckless, but at its very best, and exemplify perfectly the freedom he enjoyed that the stage of visual illusion has inevitably lost. His drama is attached solely to its actors and their acting; that, perhaps, puts it in a phrase. They carry place and time with them as they move. The modern theatre still accepts the convention that measures time more or less by a play's convenience; a half-hour stands for an hour or more, and we never question the vagary. It was no more strange to an Elizabethan audience to see a street in Rome turned, in the use made of it, to the Senate House by the drawing of a curtain and the disclosure of Cæsar's state, to find Cleopatra's Monument now on the upper stage because Antony had to be drawn up to it, later on the lower because Cleopatra's death-scene could best be played there; it would seem that they were not too astonished even when Juliet, having taken leave of Romeo on the balcony of her bedroom and watched him descend to the lower stage, the scene continuing, came down, a few lines later, to the lower stage herself, bringing, so to speak, her bedroom with her—since this apparently is what she must have done.[7] For neither Senate House, Monument nor balcony had rights and reality of their own. They existed for the convenience of the actors, whose touch gave them life, a shadowy life at most; neglected, they existed no longer.[8]

Shakespeare's stagecraft concentrates, and inevitably, upon opportunity for the actor. We think now of the plays themselves; their first public knew them by their acting; and the development of the actor's art from the agilities and funniments of the clown, and from round-mouthed rhetoric to imaginative interpreting of character by such standards as Hamlet set up for his players, was a factor in the drama's triumph that we now too often ignore. Shakespeare himself, intent more and more upon plucking out the heart of the human mystery, stimulated his actors to a poignancy and intimacy of emotional expression—still can stimulate them to it—as no other playwright has quite learned to do.

The Speaking of the Verse

His verse was, of course, his chief means to this emotional expression; and when it comes to staging the plays, the speaking of verse must be the foundation of all study. The changes of three hundred years have of themselves put difficulties in our way here; though there are some besides—as one imagines—of Shakespeare's own making. Surely his syntax must now and then have puzzled even his contemporaries. Could they have made much more than we can of Leontes'

> Affection! thy intention stabs the centre;
> Thou dost make possible things not so held,
> Communicat'st with dreams;—How can this be?
> With what's unreal thou coactive art,
> And fellow'st nothing; then, 'tis very credent
> Thou may'st co-join with something; and thou dost;
> And that beyond commission; and I find it,
> And that to the infection of my brains,
> And hardening of my brows.

The confusion of thought and intricacy of language is dramatically justified. Shakespeare is picturing a genuinely jealous man (the sort of man that Othello was *not*) in the grip of a mental epilepsy. We parse the passage and dispute its sense; spoken, as it was meant to be, in a choking torrent of passion, probably a modicum of sense slipped through, and its first hearers did not find it a mere rigmarole. But we are apt to miss even that much. Other passages, of early and late writing, may always have had as much sound as sense to them; but now, to the casual hearer, they will convey more sound than sense by far. Nor do puns mean to us what they meant to the Elizabethans, delighting in their language for its own sake. Juliet's tragic fantasia upon 'Aye' and 'I' sounds all but ridiculous, and one sympathizes with an actress hesitating to venture on it. How far, apart from the shifting of accents and the recolouring of vowels, has not the whole habit of English speech changed in these three hundred years? In the theatre it was slowing down, one fancies, throughout the eighteenth century; and in the nineteenth, as far as Shakespeare was concerned, it grew slower and slower, till on occasions one thought—even hoped—that shortly the actor would stop altogether. There may have been more than one cause; imitation of the French Augustans, the effort to make antiquated phrases understood, the increasing size of the theatres themselves would all contribute to it. The result, in any case, is disastrous. Elizabethan drama was built upon vigour and beauty of speech. The groundlings may often have deserved Shakespeare's strictures, but they would stand in discomfort for an hour or so to be stirred by the sound of verse. Some of the actors no doubt were robustious periwigpated fellows, but, equally, it was no empty ideal of acting he put into Hamlet's mouth—and Burbage's. We may suppose that at its best the mere speaking of the plays was a very brilliant thing, compared to *bel canto*, or to a pianist's virtuosity. The emotional appeal of our modern music was in it, and it could be tested by ears trained to the rich and delicate fretwork of the music of that day. Most Hamlets—not being playwrights—make a mild joke of telling us they'd as lief the town-crier spoke their lines, but we may hear in it the echo of some of Shakespeare's sorest trials.

The speaking of his verse must be studied, of course, in relation to the verse's own development. The actor must not attack its supple complexities in *Antony and Cleopatra* and *Cymbeline*, the mysterious dynamics of *Macbeth*, the nobilities of *Othello*, its final pastoral simplicities in *A Winter's Tale* and *The Tempest* without preliminary training in the lyricism, the swift brilliance and the masculine clarity of the earlier plays. A modern actor, alas, thinks it simple enough to make his way, splay-footed, through

> The cloud-capped towers, the gorgeous palaces . . .

though Berowne's

> I, forsooth, in love . . .

or one of Oberon's apostrophes will defeat him utterly. And, without an ear trained to the delicacy of the earlier work, his hearers, for their part, will never know how shamefully he is betraying the superb ease of the later. If we are to make Shakespeare our own again we must all be put to a little trouble about it. We must recapture as far as may be his lost meanings; and the sense of a phrase we *can* recapture, though instinctive emotional response to it may be a loss forever. The tunes that he writes to, the whole great art of his music-making, we can master. Actors can train their ears and tongues and can train our ears to it. We talk of lost arts. No art is ever lost while the means to it survive. Our faculties rust by disuse and by misuse are coarsened, but they quickly recover delight in a beautiful thing. Here, at any rate, is the touchstone by which all interpreting of Shakespeare the playwright must first—and last—be tried.

The Boy-Actress

MORE than one of the conditions of his theatre made this medium of accomplished speech of such worth to him. Boys played the women parts; and what could a boy bring to Juliet, Rosalind or Cleopatra beyond grace of manner and charm of speech? We have been used to women on the stage for two hundred and fifty years or more, and a boy Juliet—if the name on the programme revealed one, for nothing else might—would seem an odd fish to us; no one would risk a squeaking Cleopatra; though, as for Rosalind, through three-parts of the play a boy would have the best of it. But the parts were written for boys; not, therefore, without consideration of how boys could act them most convincingly. Hence, of course, the popularity of the heroine so disguised. The disguise was perfect; the make-believe one degree more complex, certainly, than it needs to be with us; but once you start make-believe it matters little how far you go with it; there is, indeed, some enjoyment in the make-believe itself. But, further, it is Shakespeare's constant care to demand nothing of a boy-actress that might turn to unseemliness or ridicule. He had not much taste for what is called 'domestic drama,' nor does he dose us very heavily with Doll Tearsheet, Mistress Overdone and their like. Constance mourns Arthur's loss, Lady Macduff has her little son, but no mother croons over the child in her arms. Paulina brings Hermione's baby to Leontes, it is true; but see with what tact, from this point of view, the episode is managed. And love-scenes are most carefully contrived. Romeo and Juliet are seldom alone together; never for long, but in the balcony-scene; and in this, the most famous of love-scenes, they are kept from all contact with each other. Consider *Antony and*

Cleopatra. Here is a tragedy of sex without one single scene of sexual appeal. That aspect of Cleopatra is reflected for us in talk about her; mainly by Enobarbus, who is not mealymouthed; but his famed description of her voluptuousness is given us when she has been out of our sight for several scenes. The play opens with her parting from Antony, and in their two short encounters we see her swaying him by wit, malice and with the moods of her mind. Not till the story takes its tragic plunge and sex is drowned in deeper passion are they ever intimately together; till he is brought to her dying there has been occasion for but one embrace. Contrast this with a possible Cleopatra planned to the advantage of the actress of today.

Shakespeare, artist that he was, turned this limitation to account, made loss into a gain.[9] Feminine charm—of which the modern stage makes such capital—was a medium denied him. So his men and women encounter upon a plane where their relation is made rarer and intenser by poetry, or enfranchised in a humour which surpasses more primitive love-making. And thus, perhaps, he was helped to discover that the true stuff of tragedy and of the liveliest comedy lies beyond sensual bounds. His studies of women seem often to be begun from some spiritual paces beyond the point at which a modern dramatist leaves off. Curious that not a little of the praise lavished upon the beauty and truth of them— mainly by women—may be due to their having been written to be played by boys!

Much could be said for the restoring of the celibate stage; but the argument, one fears, would be academic. Here, though, is practical counsel. Let the usurping actress remember that her sex is a liability, not an asset. The dramatist of today may refuse to exploit its allurements, but may legitimately allow for the sympathetic effect of it; though the less he does so, perhaps, the better for his play and the more gratitude the better sort of actress will show him. But Shakespeare makes no such demands, has left no blank spaces for her to fill with her charm. He asks instead for self-forgetful clarity of perception, and for a sensitive, spirited, athletic beauty of speech and conduct, which will leave prettiness and its lures at a loss, and the crudities of more Circean appeal looking very crude indeed.

The Soliloquy

THIS convention of the boy-actress may be said to give a certain remoteness to a play's acting. The soliloquy brings a compensating intimacy, and its use was an important part of Shakespeare's stagecraft. Its recognized usefulness was for the disclosing of the plot, but he soon improved upon this. Soliloquy becomes the means by which he brings us not only to a knowledge of the more secret thoughts of his characters, but into the closest emotional touch with them too. Here the platform stage helped him, as the stage of scenic illusion now defeats his purpose. But it is not altogether a question of 'realism' and the supposed obligation this lays upon a real man in a real-looking room to do nothing he would not do if the whole affair were real.

There is no escape from convention in the theatre, and all conventions can be made acceptable, though they cannot all be used indiscriminately, for they are founded in the physical conditions of the stage of their origin and are often interdependent one with another. Together they form a code, and they are as a treaty made with the audience. No article of it is to be abrogated unless we can be persuaded to consent, and upon its basis we surrender our imaginations to the playwright.

With the soliloquy upon the platform stage it is a case—as so often where convention is concerned—of extremes meeting. There is no illusion, so there is every illusion. Nothing very strange about this man, not even the dress he wears, leaning forward a little we could touch him; we are as intimate and familiar with him as it is possible to be. We agree to call him 'Hamlet', to suppose that he is where he says he is, we admit that he thinks aloud and in blank verse too. It is possible that the more we are asked to imagine the easier we find it to do. It is certain that, once our imagination is working, visual illusion will count for little in the stimulating of emotion beside this intimacy that allows the magnetism of personality full play.

There is no more important task for the producer of Shakespeare than to restore to the soliloquy its rightful place in a play's economy, and in particular to regain for it full emotional effect. We now accept the convention frigidly, the actor manoeuvres with it timidly. Banished behind footlights into that other world of illusion, the solitary self-communing figure rouses our curiosity at best. Yet further adapted to the self-contained methods of modern acting, the soliloquy has quite inevitably become a slack link in the play's action, when it should be a recurring reinforcement to its strength. Shakespeare never pinned so many dramatic fortunes to a merely utilitarian device. Time and again he may be feeling his way through a scene for a grip on his audience, and it is the soliloquy ending it that will give him—and his actor—the stranglehold. When he wishes to quicken the pulse of the action, to screw up its tension in a second or so, the soliloquy serves him well. For a parallel to its full effectiveness on Shakespeare's stage we should really look to the modern music-hall comedian getting on terms with his audience. We may measure the response to Burbage's

O, that this too too solid flesh would melt . . .

by recalling—those of us that happily can—Dan Leno
as a washerwoman, confiding domestic troubles to a
theatre full of friends, and taken unhindered to their
hearts. The problem is not really a difficult one. If we
solve the physical side of it by restoring, in essentials,
the relation between actor and audience that the intimacy of the platform stage provided, the rest should soon
solve itself.

Costume

THE problem of costume, when it arises, is a subtler one;
nor probably is it capable of any logical solution. Half
the plays can be quite appropriately dressed in the
costume of Shakespeare's own time. It is a false logic
which suggests that to match their first staging we should
dress them in the costume of ours. For with costume
goes custom and manners—or the lack of them. It may
be both a purge and a tonic to the sluggish-fancied
spectator to be shown a Prince of Denmark in coat and
trousers and a Grave-digger in a bowler hat, for remin-
der that here is a play, not a collection of ritualized
quotations. But physic is for the sick; also, there may be
less drastic cures. When archaeology took hold upon the
nineteenth-century mind it became a matter of moment
to lodge Hamlet in historic surroundings; and withers
were wrung by the anachronisms of ducats and a murder
of Gonzago, French rapiers and the rest. A needlessly
teasing difficulty; why reproduce it in terms of a young
man in a dinner jacket searching for a sword—a thing
not likely to be lying about in his modern mother's sitting
room—with which to kill Polonius, who certainly has
window curtains to hide behind instead of arras? This

gain of intimacy—with a Hamlet we might find sitting opposite at a dinner party—may well be a gain in sympathy. It was originally a great gain, a gift to Shakespeare's audience. But we pay too high a price for it.

What was the actual Elizabethan practice in this matter of costuming is not comprehensively known. We can only say safely that, as with other matters, it was neither constant, consistent, nor, from our present point of view, rational. It was based upon the use of the clothes of the time; but these might be freely and fantastically adapted to suit a particular play or advantage some character in it. Dramatic effect was probably the first consideration and the last. There were such fancy dresses as Oberon or Puck or Caliban might wear; there was always the symbolizing of royalty, and a king would wear a crown whenever he could; there was the utility of knowing Romans from Britons by sight in *Cymbeline*, the martial Roman from the effete Egyptian in *Antony and Cleopatra*, and a Scottish lord when you saw him in *Macbeth*, if we may judge by Malcolm's comment upon Rosse's appearance:

> My countryman; and yet I know him not.

Our difficulty, of course, arises mainly over the historical plays. Not over the English Histories, even so; we can dress Richard III or Henry V by the light of our own superior knowledge of what they wore, and never find it clash violently with anything Shakespeare has put on their backs or in their mouths. But when we come to Julius Cæsar plucking open his doublet, to the conspirators against him with their hats about their ears, and to Cleopatra's

> Cut my lace, Charmian.

not to mention British Imogen in her doublet and hose, we must stop and consider.

The common practice is, in these instances, to ignore the details of Shakespeare's text altogether; to dress Cæsar in his toga, Cleopatra in her habit as she lived, with never a stay-lace about her (though, truly, the costumier, let alone, will tend to get his fashion a few thousand years wrong and turn her out more like the wife of Tutankhamen); and as to Imogen and her surroundings, we do our best to compromise with skins and woad. This may be a lesser evil than presenting a Cæsar recalling Sir Walter Raleigh and a Cleopatra who would make us think of Mary Queen of Scots, but it is no solution of the problem. For the actors have to speak these lines, and if action and appearance contradict them, credibility is destroyed. And the constant credibility of the actor must be a producer's first care. Nor is this all, nor is it, perhaps, the most important thing to consider. The plays are full of reference, direct and indirect, to Elizabethan custom. They are, further, impregnated with what we call 'Renaissance feeling', some more, some less, but all to a degree. Now of this last we have a sense which is likelier to be a better help to their appreciation than any newfangled knowledge of the correct cut of Cleopatra's clothes will be! We know Iago for a Machiavellian figure (so called), and miss none of Shakespeare's intention. But if ever two men breathed the air of a sixteenth-century court, Hamlet and Claudius of Denmark do, and to relate them in habit and behaviour to the twilight figures of Saxo Grammaticus is as much a misinterpretation as any mauling of the text can be. They exist essentially doubtless—as do all the major characters of the plays—in their perennial humanity. But never let us forget the means by which this deeper truth of them is made vivid and actual. There have been better intellects than Shakespeare's, and poetry as good as his. He holds his supreme place by

his dramatist's necessary power of bringing thought and
vague emotion to the terms of action and convincing
speech; further, and far more than is often allowed, by
his peculiar gift of bringing into contribution the com-
mon-place traffic of life. However wide the spoken word
may range, there must be the actor, anchored to
the stage. However high, then, with Shakespeare, the
thought or emotion may soar, we shall always find the
transcendental set in the familiar. He keeps this balance
constantly adjusted; and, at his play's greatest moments,
when he must make most sure of our response, he will
employ the simplest means. The higher arguments of the
plays are thus kept always within range, and their rooted
humanity blossoms in a fertile upspringing of expressive
little things. Neglect or misinterpret these, the inner
wealth of Shakespeare will remain, no doubt, and we
may mine for it, but we shall have levelled his landscape
bare.

Shakespeare's own attitude in this matter of costume
and customs was as inconsistent as his practice was
casual. He knew what *his* Cæsar or Cleopatra would be
wearing and would casually drop in a reference to it.
Yet the great Romans themselves were aliens to him.
The great idea of Rome fired his imagination. Brutus,
Cassius and Antony do not turn typical Elizabethan
gentlemen; and to the end of that play he is striving to
translate Plutarch. Whenever, on the other hand, even
for a moment he has made a character all his own, he
cannot but clothe it in lively familiar detail. Cleopatra's
are the coquetries of a great lady of his own time, in
their phrasing, in the savour. When the heights of the
tragedy have to be scaled, manners will not so much
matter. But if we make her, at the play's beginning, a
pseudo-classic, languishing Oriental, we must do it in
spite of Shakespeare, not by his help. What then is the

solution of this problem, if the sight of the serpent of
old Nile in a farthingale will too dreadfully offend us?
We can compromise. Look at Tintoretto's and Paolo
Veronese's paintings of 'classic' subjects. We accept them
readily enough.

Sometimes, within the boundaries of a play, the centuries seem all at odds. *Cymbeline* need not trouble us, its
Roman Britain is pure 'once upon a time'. But in *King
Lear*, for instance, Shakespeare is at unwonted pains to
throw us back into some heathen past. Yet Edmund is
another Iago, Edgar might have been at Wittenberg with
Hamlet, and Oswald steps straight from the seventeenth-
century London streets. Here, though, the dominant
barbarism is the important thing; the setting for Goneril
and Regan, Lear's tyranny and madness, and Gloucester's blinding. To a seventeenth-century audience Oswald was so identifiable a figure that it would not matter
greatly how he dressed; the modern designer of costume
must show him up as best he may. Each play, in fine,
if it presents a problem at all, presents its own.

The Integrity of the Text

THE text, one says at first blush, can present no problem
at all. The plays should be acted as Shakespeare wrote
them—how dispute it? They should be; and it is as well,
before we discuss hard cases, to have the principle freely
admitted. Lip service enough is done it nowadays, and
Colley Cibber's *Richard III*, Tate's *Lear* and Garrick's
improvements are at the back of our bookshelves, but
we still find Messrs John Doe and Richard Roe slicing
out lines by the dozen and even a scene or so, or
chopping and changing them to suit their scenery. This
will not do. Shakespeare was not a perfect playwright;
there can be no such thing. Nor did he aim at a

mechanical perfection, but a vitality, and this he achieved. At best then, we cut and carve the body of a play to its peril. It may be robustly, but it may be very delicately organized. And we still know little enough of the laws of its existence, and some of us, perhaps, are not such very skilful surgeons; nor is any surgeon to be recommended who operates for his own convenience.

This good rule laid down, what are the exceptions that go to prove it? There is the pornographic difficulty. This is not such a stumbling block to us as it was to Bowdler, to some bright young eyes nowadays it is quite imperceptible, in fact. Yet, saving their presence, it exists; for it exists aesthetically. Shakespeare's characters often make obscene jokes. The manners of his time permitted it. The public manners of ours still do not. Now the dramatic value of a joke is to be measured by its effect upon an audience, and each is meant to make its own sort of effect. If then, instead of giving them a passing moment's amusement, it makes a thousand people uncomfortable and for the next five minutes very self-conscious, it fails of its true effect. This argument must not be stretched to cover the silliness of turning 'God' into 'Heaven' and of making Othello call Desdemona a 'wanton' (the practice, as I recollect, of the eighteen-nineties), nor to such deodorizing of *Measure for Measure* that it becomes hard to discover what all the fuss is about. If an audience cannot think of Angelo and the Duke, Pompey and Lucio, Isabella and Mistress Overdone, and themselves to boot, as fellow-creatures all, the play is not for them. Othello must call Desdemona a 'whore', and let those that do not like it leave the theatre; what have such queasy minds to do with the pity and terror of her murder and his death? Again, to make Beatrice so mealymouthed that she may not tell us how the devil is to meet her at the gates of hell, 'like an old cuckold with horns on his head', is to dress her in a crinoline, not a farthingale. But suppression of a few of the more scabrous jokes will not leave a play much the poorer; nor, one may add, will the average playgoer be much the wiser or merrier for hearing them, since they are often quite hard to understand.

Topical passages are a similar difficulty. With their savour, if not their very meaning lost, they show like dead wood in the living tree of the dialogue and are better, one would suppose, cut away. But no hard and fast rule will apply. Macbeth's porter's farmer and equivocator will never win spontaneous laughter again. But we cannot away with them, or nothing is left of the porter. Still the baffled low comedian must not, as his wont is, obscure the lines with bibulous antics. There will be that little dead spot in the play, and nothing can be done about it. Rosencrantz' reference to the 'eyrie of children' is meaningless except to the student. Is the play the poorer for the loss of it? But the logic that will take this out had better not rob us of

> Dead shepherd, now I find thy saw of might;
> Who ever loved that loved not at first sight?

And there is the strange case of

The lady of the Strachy married the yeoman of the wardrobe.

Nobody knows what it means, but everybody finds it funny when it is spoken in its place. And this has its parallels.

In general, however, better play the plays as we find them. The blue pencil is a dangerous weapon; and its use grows on a man, for it solves too many little difficulties far too easily.

Lastly, for a golden rule, whether staging or costuming or cutting is in question, and a comprehensive creed, a producer might well pin this on his wall: Gain Shakespeare's effects by Shakespeare's means when you can; for, plainly, this will be the better way. But gain Shakespeare's effects; and it is your business to discern them.

1927

Notes

1 But it should not be forgotten that Sir Herbert Tree, happy in the orthodoxy of public favour, welcomed the heretic Mr Poel more than once to a share in his Shakespeare Festivals.

2 I do not deal in general therefore with certain vexed questions, such as act-division, which still need to be looked at, I think, in the light of the particular play.

3 I remember a most intelligent reader of a modern play missing the whole point of a scene through which the chief character was to sit conspicuously and eloquently silent. He counted only with the written dialogue. I remember, when I thought I knew *King Lear* well enough, being amazed at the effect, all dialogue apart, of the mere meeting, when I saw it, of blind Gloucester and mad Lear.

4 Though, in a sense, there was no first performance of *Hamlet*. And doubtless many of the audience for Shakespeare's new version of the old play only thought he had spoiled a good story of murder and revenge by adding too much talk to it.

5 Unless it may be said that we learn in the scene after whereabouts he *was*.

6 And in *Coriolanus*, which probably postdates *Antony and Cleopatra*, with Marcius' 'A goodly city is this Antium,' we are back to the barely informative. It serves Shakespeare's purpose; he asks no more.

7 I fancy, though, that the later Shakespeare would have thought this a clumsy device.

8 How far this is true of other dramatists than Shakespeare I do not pretend to say; nor how far, with him, the influence of the private theatre, making undoubtedly towards the scenic stage

and (much later) for illusion, did not modify his practice, when he had that stage to consider. A question, again, for the bibliographers and historians.

9 There is no evidence, of course, that he felt it a loss, no such reference to the insufficiency of the boy-actress as there is to the overself-sufficiency of the clown. Women did appear in the Masques, if only to dance, so the gulf to be bridged was not a broad one. But the Elizabethan was as shocked by the notion of women appearing upon the public stage as the Chinese playgoer is today.

Macbeth

TO pitch upon an informing epithet, *Macbeth* is the starkest of the great tragedies. It is the least discursive, even less so than *Othello*. With *Othello* it is the most forthright in its action; and this we should expect, for it is the tragedy of unchecked will, even as *Hamlet* is the tragedy of indecision. It is cold and harsh and unrelenting. If Shakespeare's mind was ever plagued by the doctrine of hell hereafter, this play might well be his comment on it. He puts hell here. Macbeth the man is a study in self-damnation. 'Hell is murky,' says the wretched woman in her sleep, and she may have further yet to go on to find it. But he ends as a soulless man, a beast, chained to a stake and slaughtered like a beast.

So much, if it be allowed, for general guidance in picturing the play.

The Text

We meet at once with an unusual difficulty. For long, producers of the plays have been mercilessly hacking at Shakespeare's authentic work, though the custom at last is losing credit. But in *Macbeth*, however conscientious we may be, there will be forced on us, apparently, work which is not his at all.

Hecate may be ruled out with hardly a second thought. If this be not true Middleton, it is at least true twaddle, and Shakespeare—though he had his lapses—was not in a twaddling mood when he wrote *Macbeth*.

The chief difficulty is with the play's opening. Good opinion holds that we do not meet Shakespeare's true text till Macbeth's own entrance with

So foul and fair a day I have not seen.

If this be so, should the producer boldly begin here? It will make an interesting and very possible, and indeed a most dramatic, beginning. It will be in line with the forthrightness of the play's whole action. We should have this significant note struck at once by the protagonist; the weird sisters would suddenly and silently appear, as unexpectedly to us as to him, and the main theme would be opened with dignity and directness. The experiment might be well worth trying. But, almost certainly, this was not Shakespeare's beginning. Precedent is against it. The technique of *Richard II* and *Richard III* was far behind him; and, even though in the late-written *Antony and Cleopatra* there are but ten lines to be spoken before the chief characters appear, the difference between this and the speaking of the very first word of the play is, in theatrical effect, a great one.

On the other hand it is hardly more likely that he began with the witches.[1] Apart from such an opening being un-Shakespearean, the lines themselves are as little like Shakespeare as Hecate is, and have indeed all the tang of the Hecate lines. Critical glorification of the scene and its supposed purpose has not, of course, been wanting. But this mainly belongs to the class of commentary that deals with Norns and Shakespeare's knowledge of Northern mythology and the like, and need not trouble the simple theatrical mind, to whom a play must be first and even last a play. The scene—as better and sterner critical authority allows—is a poor scene and a pointless scene. And Shakespeare did not, at any rate, begin his plays with superfluities. For all the offence to stage tradition, therefore, it may well be omitted.

Now comes the question of Scene ii. This, we may hazard, does at least stand for Shakespeare's beginning.

That the lines themselves have been mauled is obvious, whether by Middleton, some stage-manager, or the compositor. There is possibly matter missing. Even allowing for some desired effect of the confusion of battle and rebellion, the scene has not that expository clearness which is one of the hall-marks of true Shakespeare.[2] As Shakespeare wrote it, probably it was a better scene. But if, as we have it, it represents something of his intention, the safe plan is perhaps to take it as the play's beginning. It at least makes a fair start.

As to Scene iii Shakespeare may well have begun it with the weird sisters. But the present opening seems spurious, and it is quite out of key with the more authentic part of the scene. There is much to be said for boldly omitting it, and beginning, as aforesaid, with the entrance of Macbeth and Banquo.

This will dispose of the more serious textual difficulties. The porter's scene, both on the count of stagecraft[3] and on the aesthetic count, is surely genuine, and we have hardly sufficient cause to discard lines 37—59 of the scene between Lady Macduff and the child, though one must own to a suspicion of them.[4]

The entrance (Act IV, Scene iii) of the English doctor and the speech about the King's Evil is another matter. No doubt this is Shakespeare's work. It is equally obvious that he wrote it to please King James I, whom neither he nor we can any longer hope to please. But, upon kindred grounds, too much slashing may be done, and has been done. We must bring to the seeing of Shakespeare a certain historical sense. Besides, the episode has its dramatic value too. It helps to create—and there is little to do this—the benevolent atmosphere of the English court for a contrast with the description of Scotland in her agony. Certainly these twenty-two lines should be retained.

Staging and Directing

Upon a stage of typical Elizabethan equipment no difficulty of presentation need, of course, occur. And indications for the use of outer, inner and upper stage—though arguable occasionally—are not on the whole hard to follow. Until we reach

Enter Macbeth's wife alone with a letter,

the action is well enough suited to the outer stage. The weird sisters, at the Globe, *may* have appeared in the gallery. But Macbeth's 'Into the air' when they vanish, is no stronger evidence of this than is Banquo's 'The earth hath bubbles' that they appeared on the ground. The dramatic effect, though, will surely be greater if they do actually stop the way upon that imaginary blasted heath.

Duncan's second scene could conceivably employ the inner stage; but then Lady Macbeth's first scene must be played above; and this seems, on the whole, an unlikely arrangement;—though a certain effect would then be gained by her descent later to welcome Duncan. But her first talk with Macbeth is an intimate one, and that argues rather the use of the inner stage.

Act I Scene vii, might well be played on the outer stage; the procession of the

Sewer and divers servants with dishes and service

sufficing to mark passage of time and change of place. Still—the chamber where Duncan was supping being thought of as below—an effect could be gained by the drawing back of the inner stage curtains and the use by Macbeth and Lady Macbeth of the actual door of the inner stage as the chamber door. This would somewhat confine their scene together, perhaps to its advantage, and would also allow the lapse of time before Act II to be emphasised by the redrawing of the curtains.

Then for Act II the outer and—as I shall suggest—the upper stages will suffice. Macbeth's 'As I descended' is evidence that Duncan's sleeping chamber is imagined above. If we presume the curtains of an inner upper stage to be drawn close, there is no need for actual going up and down during the murder, and Lady Macbeth's quick re-entrance after her exit with the daggers would not be delayed. But it will be noticed that between Macduff's

> I'll make so bold to call

and his re-entrance after the discovery twelve lines are spoken. This presumably leaves ample time for him to mount to the upper stage. Moreover, the effect of his re-entrance through the closed curtains and of his delivering,

> O horror! horror! horror!

from the gallery will be very striking. The other characters would then assemble there, and there the rest of the scene would be played. One may suggest that what Shakespeare visualised was a number of people rushing out on the landing at the sound of the alarm bell, as they would in any country house to-day. They should be more or less in their night attire. This is connoted by

> And when we have our naked frailties hid;

and

> Let's briefly put on manly readiness
> And meet i' the hall together,

is fully pointed by situating the scene thus. It would be possible too—and effective—for Malcolm and Donalbain after

Let's away; our tears are not yet brew'd,

to descend to the lower stage and finish the scene there. The last three speeches would then seem, as they should, a postscript to the rest, rather than an anti-climax.

Act III, Scene i, seems planned for the outer stage. Scene ii could be played there as well, but it might be more effective on the inner stage. The stage-manager's difficulty would lie in the setting of the banquet for Scene iv. But this should not trouble him. And unless there is to be a long pause before Act IV (and it should be noted that the scene between Lenox and another lord obviates any) he would have to be about as quick in clearing it away and setting the cauldron for the weird sisters. Scenes iii and vi are on the outer stage, of course. And for Scene iv the outer and inner stages are used together. Scene v is to be counted apocryphal.

The arrangement for Act IV is obvious; an inner scene and two outer scenes to follow.

In Act V the direct alternation of inner and outer scenes is arguably complete. But the stage directions for Scene vii suggest that, by the time of their insertion, at any rate, some more complex arrangement had been devised. Young Siward is slain, but there is no apparent provision for removing the body.[5] There is also the direction for Macbeth and Macduff,

Exeunt fighting. Alarums.

and immediately,

Enter fighting and Macbeth slain.

Then, without a pause, and, again with no provision for the removal of the body,

Retreat, flourish. Enter with drum and colours Malcolm . . .

And twenty-four lines later comes,

Enter Macduff with Macbeth's head.

We may be fairly certain that the play is meant to end
on the lower stage. If Macduff and Macbeth are to have
a good fight, this—or at least the best part of it—should
take place on the lower stage too. Now the double stage
direction will be made clear if they can leave the lower
stage fighting, and re-appear in the gallery.[6] If Macbeth
is killed on the inner upper stage the drawing of its
curtain would conceal his body. And if young Siward
had been killed there too, there would be no pressing
necessity for the removal of his. If then we may imagine,
besides, the curtains of the inner lower stage drawn back
and both outer and inner stages in use, the directions
for the whole scene could read thus:

Alarums. Enter Macbeth above.

MACBETH. They have tied me to a stake; I cannot fly ...

*Enter young Siward; either directly on the upper stage, or by crossing
the lower stage from (say) the left door.*[7]

Alarums. Enter Macduff below by left door.

MACDUFF. That way the noise is ...

Exit by right door ...

Enter Malcolm and old Siward below by left door.

SIWARD. Enter, sir, the castle.

Exeunt through inner stage.

Alarum. Enter Macbeth below by right door.

MACBETH. Why should I play the Roman fool ...

Enter Macduff below by right door. ...

Exeunt fighting, either by right door, or, possibly, through inner stage.
Alarums. Re-enter fighting on upper stage. Retreat. Flourish. Enter
Malcolm, etc., in procession through inner stage.

This scheme would further suggest that Scene V might
be played on the upper stage. The opening line

Hang out our banners on the outward walls,

gives some colour to the idea. But it is not a scene wholly
of action. It contains the more or less reflective

To-morrow, and to-morrow, and to-morrow;[8]

and much would depend upon the immediacy of touch
with the audience that such a position gave to the actor.
That again would largely depend upon particularities of
the theatre's construction. This is the sort of consideration that must often have ruled in or out the employ-
ment of the upper stage.

With regard to any scheme of staging other than the
Elizabethan one can here but elaborate a little the
general principles laid down already for a more liberal
treatment of the plays. Presumably such a scheme would
hang to some extent upon decorative effect. That it must
never clog the action is axiomatic. As to the service it
can render to this particular play; it can perhaps point
the action by reinforcing the effect of swift movement
through the earlier scenes of preparation and increasing
tension to the murder of Duncan and its discovery.[9] It
can perhaps do something to point the downward rush
towards the play's end, that counterbalances the opening
rise in Macbeth's fortune. It can give us something of
the barbaric grandeur with which we may suppose Macbeth would emphasise his regality. It can no doubt
sharpen the contrast—though the play itself provides this
by one stroke after another—between the court, the

sights that the weird sisters show, the simplicity of Macduff's home, the kindly security of England and the unnatural strain of that scene of tragic twilight through which Lady Macbeth's tortured spirit drifts towards death.

It will be convenient to speak here of the act division of the play, for this is bound to affect the consideration of anything that can be called scenery. Elsewhere, in dealing with the plays generally, it has been suggested that we need not feel bound by the Folio's arbitrary division of each play into five acts, nor at any rate to the observance of an interval at the end of each. And there are some signs in this play at least that in practice this particular division was not originally observed.

The play, in the light of its story, falls into three parts. Acts I and II form the first and stand for the achievement of Macbeth's ambition. Act III, with the two first scenes of Act IV, form a second, which shows his wielding of power. From thence to the end we see the process of retribution. There are dramatic advantages in this arrangement.[10]

This first part is undeniably a unit of action; and in only one place does a halt seem to be called: at the end of Act I. Here a pause will have value, a pause, that is to say, which an audience can sit through in expectant silence. But a break in the tension, such as must be made by the usual inter-act disturbance and conversation, will be equally disastrous. What is wanted dramatically is, so to speak, a few moments' vacancy, in which the vibrations of the strenuous scene that ends with

> ... I am settled and bend up
> Each corporal agent to this terrible feat.
> Away, and mock the time with fairest show;
> False face must hide what the false heart doth know.

may disperse, and the audience grow sensitive to the quiet opening of Banquo's

> How goes the night, boy?

If we are to imagine that the lights of the banqueting-chamber have been visible, or any snatches of music or talk heard coming from it, a slow darkening and silencing of these might gain the effect.

The second part, again, is a dramatic unit. And, if it seems to end with a comparatively unimportant scene,[11] it must be remembered that it is the murder of Lady Macduff and his son which precipitates Macduff's vengeance. This therefore leads us directly on to the third part.

It may be said that Act IV as it stands in the Folio is a better gathering of scenes. But there is this against it. Act IV, Scene iii (between Malcolm, Macduff and Rosse), is the hardest in the play to make interesting in its entirety, and it gets its best chance by being made an opening scene. Again, the sleep-walking scene, which, if Act IV of the Folio is left intact, must begin Act V, is at a grave disadvantage so placed, with its audience quite unkeyed to its necessarily subdued tone. On the other hand, the close connection of the two has great value. The contrast between Macduff and Malcolm's manly tune and the whisperings of the doctor and the waiting gentlewoman and the slumbery agitation that follows is well worth emphasising.

Let us come back to the question of the play's decoration. The barbaric splendour of Macbeth's court! That is the dangerous sort of phrase that slips into the mind when Shakespeare sets one's imagination free. The practical danger will lie, of course, in any attempt to capitalize this imagination in such extrinsic things as scenery and clothes, lights and music. We may make for safety by confining ourselves to such use of these things as Shakespeare himself had. If this appears an ignoble timidity, we must then at least see that they do not conflict with things intrinsic to the play. This principle will not be disputed perhaps, but pitfalls in practice are many and unexpected. From some of the commonly less observed of them, however, *Macbeth* is freer than most of the plays.

The question of illusionary scenery need not be argued. Woe betide the painter upon canvas who will compete with

> This castle hath a pleasant seat; the air
> Nimbly and sweetly recommends itself
> Unto our gentle senses.
>   This guest of summer,
> The temple-haunting martlet, does approve
> By his lov'd mansionry that the heaven's breath
> Smells wooingly here; no jutty, frieze,
> Buttress, nor coign of vantage, but this bird
> Hath made his pendent bed and procreant cradle:
> Where they most breed and haunt, I have observ'd
> The air is delicate;

or with

> The west yet glimmers with some streaks of day:
> Now spurs the lated traveller apace,
> To gain the timely inn.

But if we are brought to ask, how did Shakespeare—the bare equipment of his theatre apart—visualize the setting of his play, there is evidence in the writing that his sense of period and place differed not so greatly from ours—if we are not too well informed in archaeology. He may, for instance, have passed blasted heaths between London and Stratford; and so, a very little further afield, may we. But is it the general colouring of the verse rather than any particular passages that seems to show Shakespeare's vision of a wilder country than his own; strange, yet not so strange to him that, for reasons of practical artistry, the difference was better ignored. Much of this verse-colouring no doubt concerns the characters more than their habitat. Even so, there is still an overplus for the broader effect.

That Shakespeare imagined—and that his actors wore—an unusual costume is shown by Malcolm's line upon Rosse's approach,

> My countryman; but yet I know him not.

Rosse may actually have worn nothing more symbolic of Scotland than a bonnet and a claymore, but the admission is enough.

Press too far on this path, though, and the pitfalls begin. Macbeth's castle, as we have seen, had the conveniences of the Globe Theatre; and the further suggestions of the night of the murder are rather of houses and habits familiar to that audience than of Scotland in the year A.D. 1000. Bells ring, people get on their nightgowns,[12] and the porter makes topical jokes. And though in the matter of costume we have neither Cleopatra's 'Cut my lace, Charmian,' to contend with, nor the subtler incongruities which crop out when we try to present the Italianate Claudius of Denmark as half a Viking, or Cloten, the player at bowls and provider of serenades, as an ancient Briton, in *Macbeth*, too, archaeology will insensibly undo us.

The decorator, then, of this particular tragedy may count himself lucky to be as untrammelled as he is, and so little plagued by such anachronisms (mostly of the modern mind's creating) as cripple an interpretation of the more strictly historical plays. Let him strike, may we suggest, an agreement with producer and actors upon the mood of the play, and help to project *that* into its environing and equipment; as, within these covers, Mr Charles Ricketts has now alone so admirably done.[13]

Music

Little enough use is, or well can be, made of music. There are few plays of Shakespeare in which this amenity—and all other such—is so sternly repressed. Hence, no doubt, Middleton's incursion with his songs and dances. It looks, however, as if the twice repeated inclusion of 'Ho-boyes' in the directions for Duncan's arrival at Inverness might be Shakespearean enough, and may indicate a festivity of welcome.[14] If so, it is just such a good stroke of irony as we should expect. The second direction may also indicate music during the banquet. It may; one can hardly say more. Here is a question of taste and matter for experiment. Certainly the horror of the scene for which Macbeth has left the chamber will be strengthened by a background of happy hospitality.[15] The contrast with the stillness to come and the fact that the scene which follows will call mainly for the same two actors in the same mood, should also be reckoned with. But it must be a distant background, no doubt.

Ho-boyes are noted again for the *Show of eight kings*, Banquo's descendants. And the recalling here by such unobtrusive means of Duncan's ceremonious welcome at Inverness would be valuable.

For Macbeth's kingship the Folio gives *A sennet sounded*, and no more.

But the drums, alarums, retreat and flourish of the battlefield must be considered. They are not meant to be mere noises. Just as the colours carried symbolized an army, so did these sounds symbolize upon that 'unrealistic' stage the varying phases of a battle. Treated as music they can be made symbolic; and though nowadays we have forgotten the alphabet of the convention, it is an easy one to re-learn. There is emotional value, too, in the sound of the trumpet. We need no learning to be stirred by that.

The Casting of the Parts

There will be the perennial difficulty of weighing the physical fitness or, it may be, the emotional power, of actors against their intellectual capacity. There can be no making of rules in the matter. To say that Macbeth must look like this or like that is to treat the play as a waxwork show. At the other extreme, to suppose that capacity to understand includes ability to express, is to confuse theatre with class-room. One may dogmatize a little upon temperament. One may—indeed one must— estimate the sheer, crude strength that a man needs to last out in the acting of such a part as Macbeth. One may sometimes say of any part or of any passage: This *cannot* be so. The rest is immediate judgment.

It is interesting to recall that the actress most identified in public memory with Lady Macbeth sinned most, and perforce, against her own notion of the part. Mrs Siddons says she thought of the woman as 'fair, feminine, nay, perhaps even fragile'. But—in her famous years at least—she played her like an avenging goddess. Without doubt she builded worse than she knew; and—this is the pity of it—the tradition of her superhuman presence has misguided many a performance since. Let us set aside the fact that Shakespeare had a boy of seventeen to play for him instead of a woman of forty, 'massive and concrete'—to quote a classic criticism of quite another performance—and see simply what demands the text makes. The first is surely for swiftness of method. Macbeth at the outset is the hanger-back, his wife is the speeder on. She is the gadfly stinging him to action. He will not 'catch the nearest way'; the night's great business must be put into her 'despatch'. Such small hints, though, are nothing beside the sweep of purpose that informs her every line in these scenes; and the actress who plays them slowly yields her prime function in the play's action.[16] And swiftness will imply lightness of touch, though neither, needless to say, must connote hurry. There is certainly no textual evidence that Lady Macbeth was physically fragile. For obvious reasons a dramatist does not crib, cabin and confine the realization of his work in such a way.[17] But the dramatic gain in making her so is hardly disputable. The effect of the 'undaunted spirit' is doubled if we marvel that so frail a body can contain it. There will be an appropriate beauty in her fainting. A small matter this; but Shakespeare himself has touched in the incident so sparely that if it is not rightly done on the very stroke there is no dialogue or extra circumstance by which an error can be retrieved. And the thin-drawn tragedy of her end will be deepened.

We should see her even physically weighed down with the crown and robes that she struck for. When

> Our hostess keeps her state,

it should seem as if the lonely, wan figure upon the throne had no strength left to move. She does make one amazing effort to save Macbeth from himself and from discovery.

> Are you a man? . . . O proper stuff!
> This is the very painting of your fear . . .
> Fie, for shame! . . .

Think of this, good peers, but as a thing of custom . . .
I pray you speak not; he grows worse and worse.

This is the old fire upflaring. But it exhausts her. When
the two are left alone she can say no more, do no more.

You lack the season of all natures, sleep .

What an emptiness of hope and help underlies the
phrase! He, at heart as hopeless, responds with the
bravado of

Come, we'll to sleep.

Later it will be made very clear what sort of seasoning
sleep brings to her. And when next we see her in
slumbery agitation we should hardly be sure, but for the
concern of the doctor and her gentlewoman, whether
this wraith that sighs and mutters and drifts away is still
a living creature or no.[18]

Then there is the commonplace but important consideration of the contrast with Macbeth. About him there
must be something colossal; and if this primary effect
cannot be obtained by direct means, every indirect
resource must be used to suggest it. Not that mere
physical bulk will avail. But Macbeth is a valiant man
and, even before he becomes king, of an almost royal
demeanour. He treats Duncan with a certain stiff dignity
and Banquo with condescension. Only his wife knows
the weakness that his high manner hides. And when he
is king this demeanour is stamped even more deeply
upon him. It has the greater effect because he keeps
alone. Does he do so because he needs now to assert his
will upon himself? Needs apart, he appears to find some
satisfaction in exercising it on others. The length of the
scene with Banquo's murderers has puzzled commentators. But is it not as if Macbeth, not content to give the

fellows their orders and their pay, wanted to subdue their wills? One sees him pacing the floor and weaving words like spells round the two wretches, stopping every now and then to eye them hard and close. First he wants, above all, to commit them to a deeper guilt towards Banquo. This shows later in his cry of

> Thou canst not say I did it.

Duncan might justly fill his dreams. But Banquo was their enemy too, they hated him, they had done the deed: why then should he be haunted?

From the time we first see him as king, the figure of the man grows huger, harsher and gaunter. He loves his wife still. It is partly his very love that makes him keep himself from her; why should he damn her deeper with a share of the guilt to come?[19] Partly, no doubt, it is that he knows she is broken and useless. One of the few strokes of pathos that are let soften the grimness of the tragedy is Lady Macbeth's wan effort to get near enough to the tortured man to comfort him, but the royal robes, stiff on their bodies—stiff as with caked blood—seem to keep them apart. He has grown a stranger to her, who was once the inspiration of all he did![20] He treats her like a child:

> Be innocent of the knowledge, dearest chuck,
> Till thou applaud the deed.

Like an innocent child he cannot treat her. It is worth noting that, in this scene, Macbeth's mind is all upon the ill-powers of Nature—upon the powers that the weird sisters wield—as if it were their fellowship he now felt the need of.

We should mark, too, the bravery—and more than bravery—with which, later, he confronts the ghost. His nerves may give way, but he will not be the victim of his nerves. He dares it to come again, he drinks again to Banquo, his voice rises to the toast, clear, hearty, defiant. He means to test himself, to pit himself against every consequence of his deeds. 'Dare' is the note for all these passages. And, though he trembles still, it would seem that he wins; so to read,

> Hence, horrible shadow! Unreal mockery, hence!

and the ghost's vanishing.

Having outfaced this, he commits himself, from now on, to murder without scruple. And, as he loses humanity, he seems somehow to grow in physical strength. The power that went to make him man now goes to make him doubly brute, till, at the end, tied to a stake, he fights and dies like a wild beast indeed; and not till we see his severed head can we be sure that the evil life is out of him.

The actor of Macbeth has a mighty task. He must start at a pitch high enough to overtop his fellows; and the first part of the play will tax his judgment in balancing strength and weakness, conscience and ill ambition.[21] Between the entrance as king and that line which looks to nethermost hell,

> We are yet but young in deed,

he has to carry his audience with him into such a world as Dante drew, where the spirit of man moves downward

> per l' aere amaro e sozzo.

And in these scenes the technique of the play's writing, as it concerns the two chief characters, changes somewhat; and Shakespeare by his own great achievement adds to his interpreters' difficulties even while he offers them great chance of achievement too. For set the swift flow of the verse and the comparative directness and simplicity of the thoughts in the first part of the play beside this picture of the haunted desert of their souls, in which we are now to watch these two creatures moving, and note what a change of method is dictated to the actors for its realization.

Macbeth's soliloquy in Act III, Scene i, and Lady Macbeth's four lines spoken alone in the following scene have clarity enough. But the rest of the dialogue is often but a mask behind which their minds are moving. Quite naturally, quite dramatically. Before they could talk freely to each other, these two. Now they cannot, and that in itself would begin their mutual tragedy. Sometimes the lines seem to carry echoes of a meaning which the speaker himself only dimly divines.

> It will have blood; they say blood will have blood;

and

> Strange things I have in head that will to hand,
> Which must be acted ere they may be scanned.

Here is more for the actor to do than to speak words, however expressively.

And, besides, there is all the unwritten motion of the play, the smiling menace to Banquo, the unspoken threat to the courtiers if they heed the 'strange inventions' that Malcolm and Donalbain are spreading abroad, the varied undercurrents during the banquet scene. In all these attributes to the text the actor must, so to speak, clothe himself; yet, be it ever remembered that he must not *depreciate* the play's chief means of expression, the winged words and the verse that charges them with emotion.

From here to the play's end the part of Macbeth may be held to suffer somewhat from Shakespeare's plan of it inevitably lodging him in a dilemma. He means to brutalize the man, but a man so brutalized becomes less capable of poetic expression. The wild vigour with which the weird sisters are conjured comes naturally enough. But later, is not Shakespeare apt to leap this difficulty? Macbeth must moralize; so be it. But the sensibility of

> I have liv'd long enough,

and

> I 'gin to be aweary of the sun,

does not go over well in close conjunction with

> I'll fight till from my bones my flesh be hack'd.

It is not that the inconsistency could not be explained away. It is not even that there is in reality any inconsistency at all. It is rather that, within the narrow limits of drama at least, a character cannot be effectively developed in two directions at once. Shakespeare is hurrying Macbeth, defiant to the last, towards a hopeless doom. It is true that this quick shifting of mind in a man whose whole moral nature is in collapse, is a recognizable thing. But, with so little more to do to the character, Shakespeare has, for the sake of space perhaps, done some of it rather arbitrarily; and these passages—beautiful as they are, and, indeed, in their very beauty—are apt, straightforwardly interpreted, to seem to lie dead in the living body of the rest. Either so, or they require such subtle rendering as in itself is out of place.

When his wife is in question we do quite naturally catch the echo of Macbeth's earlier feelings for her, when he still could feel. The doctor tells him that she is

> . . . troubled with thick-coming fancies

That keep her from her rest,

and his

Cure her of that

comes, though hollowly, from his heart. But at once
there follows the mocking

> Canst thou not minister to a mind diseased?

When he hears she is dead, by instinct he turns back
silently to that earlier self to find his response. But there
is none. He almost shrugs.

> She should have died hereafter.

Then, perhaps, he might have felt something, found
some meaning in her loss. But now his only relief is to
burst into a rage of pessimism. Whatever meaning has
this life at all?

> It is a tale
> Told by an idiot, full of sound and fury,
> Signifying nothing.

It will be safe to suggest to most actors that in this
last section of the play they should set themselves above
all to avoid sententiousness. Macbeth sententious!

With regard to Banquo one can hardly do better
than—with the thanks due for this as for so much else
in the study of Shakespeare—quote Professor Bradley's
analysis of his character.

'... Banquo is evidently a bold man, probably an
ambitious one, and certainly has no lurking guilt in his
ambition.'

'... he would repel the "cursed thoughts" [that the
weird sisters had prompted in him]; and they are mere
thoughts, not intentions. But still they are "thoughts",
something more, probably, than mere recollections; and
they bring with them an undefined sense of guilt. The
poison has begun to work. [After the murder] ... we

may be pretty sure that he suspects the truth at once ...
He is profoundly shocked, full of indignation, and deter-
mined to play the part of a brave and honest man.

'But he plays no such part. When next we see him,
on the last day of his life, we find that he has yielded
to evil. The witches and his own ambition have con-
quered him. He alone of the lords knew of the
prophecies, but he has said nothing of them. He has
acquiesced in Macbeth's accession, and in the official
theory that Duncan's sons had suborned the chamber-
lains to murder him. ... He has, not formally but in
effect, "cloven to" Macbeth's "consent"; he is knit to
him by "a most indissoluble tie". ... And his soliloquy
tells us why:

> Thou hast it now: King, Cawdor, Glamis, all,
> As the weird women promised, and, I fear,
> Thou play'dst most foully for't: yet it was said
> It should not stand in thy posterity,
> But that myself should be the root and father
> Of many kings. If there come truth from them—
> As upon thee, Macbeth, their speeches shine—
> Why, by the verities on thee made good
> May they not be my oracles as well,
> And set me up in hope? But hush! no more.

This "hush! no more" is not the dismissal of "cursed
thoughts": it only means that he hears the trumpets
announcing the entrance of the King and Queen. His
punishment comes swiftly, much more swiftly than Macbeth's, and saves him from any further fall.'

What better guidance could producer or actor ask?

The occasion of Macduff's introduction to the play
should be noted. He appears in Duncan's train at Inverness, but does not speak. The discovery of the murder,
however, is given to him. And it is obvious that Shake-

speare requires a voice to ring out clear, candid and unafraid with

> O horror! horror! horror! Tongue nor heart
> Cannot conceive nor name thee!

His voice should be like light breaking in—even though it be a stormy sunrise. This extreme contrast with what has gone before is a very necessary effect. And candour is Macduff's keynote. He is placed in direct contrast to Macbeth; he stands, moreover, in blunt relief against the other tactful courtiers. Shakespeare is sparing of material in this play, but here is enough, and it can be given point to. The immediate

> Wherefore did you so?

when Macbeth lets out that he has killed the grooms, followed by observant silence, is worth, well acted and well arranged, a dozen expository speeches. By his retort to the pliant Rosse's

> Will you to Scone?
>   No, cousin, I'll to Fife,

any sufficient actor can so fix the character and its dramatic purpose in our memory that his re-appearance even after many scenes will have full importance.

The scene in England needs as careful handling as any in the play and is commonly held not to repay the care; most producers hack at its text mercilessly. But this—principles apart—is penny-wise policy. The scene is the starting-point of the play's counter-action, and everything should be done to enhance its importance. Malcolm is to be king of Scotland. He is thought by most actors an ungrateful part, but Shakespeare at least did not leave him a nonentity. It will be useful to enquire why this scene is, as it is, a long level of verse, with its thoughts and emotions, till toward the end, rather cata-logued than spontaneously springing. One simple expla-nation is that at this point in the play's writing Shakespeare was tired—as well he might be, after what had come before—but had to push on somehow. And we know that he all but transcribed a considerable passage from Holinshed. In the result the scene has been accounted dull—as dull, the irreverent might protest, as the virtue it chronicles. But we must look carefully to the playwright's intention. He needed for his audience, if not for himself, a breathing-space in which to recover from the shaking effects of the tragedy as he had so far developed it, and to prepare for the final rush of events. For this purpose a short scene would not suffice. He had already provided in the scene between Rosse, the old man and Macduff, and in the scene between Lenox and another lord, intervals of calm contrast with the bloody business of the play's main action. And it is, incidentally, most important to give these scenes their full value, to let the music of their smoother verse bring some relief to our ear, and the irony of their content—for the contrast is not a violent one—set our thoughts to work after our emotion has been so played upon.

But now neither would an unemotional scene suffice. Most certainly Scotland is not to be saved by the like of the cool time-serving Rosse and Lenox. They may be well-intentioned men enough. But Macduff marks even their greatest worth at such a time (and Malcolm's, as he thinks) with

> Great tyranny, lay thou thy basis sure,
> For goodness dares not check thee!

That Malcolm might be what his self-accusation would make him, that Macduff might be Macbeth's spy, that each then should turn from the other in loathing, and that Macduff should not be too easily convinced of the truth—all this is necessary as a solid foundation for the moral dominance of the rest of the play by these two. And the whole matter must be given space and weight to the measure of its importance. There is a formalism in the writing, true; and it may be more formal than Shakespeare could and would have made it at a more favourable moment. But even in the formalism there is significance. Malcolm is meant to be a young man who is deliberately virtuous, level-headed moreover, and as-tute. And however unheroic such a figure may seem to the romantically-minded playgoer, Shakespeare will have it that this is the man to save Scotland. Given an actor of the right authority for Malcolm, the scene can be made interesting enough. A thing in it to make clear and stress carefully is the opposition between the natures of the two men and their ways of approach to each other: Macduff outspoken; Malcolm reserved, over-cau-tious at first, though never cold. From its beginning, indeed, the scene is, beneath the surface, well charged with emotion. And Macduff's line,

> Such welcome and unwelcome things at once
> 'Tis hard to reconcile,

which one has often heard an actor speak with an air of tame puzzlement, is really the passionate, half-choked utterance of a man still torn between hope and despair.

We have before noted the value of the little interlude of the doctor's entrance and the speech about the King's Evil. And the rest of the scene is plain sailing.[22]

Rosse must be carefully cast. It is a 'stock-company' tradition that this part was the last insult that could be offered to a responsible actor. On the other hand pages have been written by an ingenious gentleman to dem-onstrate that he is the motive force and the real villain of the play. To bring this home in performance, he would, one fears, have to be accompanied throughout by an explanatory chorus. But he is, in truth, a not uninteresting figure. The part is threaded more consecutively through the play than any other. Confronted with each catastrophe, Rosse stands emotionally untouched. He stands, indeed, as a kind of silent or smoothly speaking and cynical chorus to the tragic happenings. With great matter in hand, Shakespeare is, as we have noticed, thrifty in the writing of his minor parts; in this play thriftier perhaps than in any other. Unless, therefore, the producer so wills and most carefully contrives, nothing much can be made of the part. It is a negative figure. But that is its significance, and a most valuable one. And with care and intelligent acting this 'ever-gentle' gentleman, with his

> Alas, the day,

his

> Gentlemen, rise, his highness is not well,

his

> You must have patience, madam,

his admirable tact when he brings the news to Macduff of his children's and wife's slaughter, his smooth sympathy with Siward for his son's death, may be made very distinctive.[23] He is more of a 'Renaissance' figure than the others. He is, in the old sense of the word, a politician. He is the play's taciturn *raisonneur*.

The part of Lady Macduff is in itself very easily effective; the child's part, mettlesomely played, even more so. The only trouble with the scene can be that it is too effective; within three or four minutes, that is to say, a direful catastrophe is precipitated upon two characters with whom we are hardly acquainted, and without, therefore, sufficient aesthetic cause. Shakespeare helps us over this difficulty by giving scope for a well-coloured, positive personality; and this should determine a Lady Macduff's casting. With her first line she can make herself sufficiently known to the audience:

What had he done to make him fly the land?

It is important, too, that the killing of the child should be done very deliberately. The thing is so abhorrent that we are apt to try and gloss it over in action. This is a mistake. The dramatic enormity is belittled by the open-eyed, heroic readiness with which the child faces death. This heroism strikes the note upon which the scene must end.

To pass upon some details. There is a tradition—one of those quite unreliable stage traditions—which speaks of the porter as the Drunken Porter, and makes him in appearance a candidate for an inebriates' home. For such a painful effort at comedy Shakespeare gives us no warrant. Truly the porter had been carousing till the second cock, and no doubt the news of the victory and the king's visit made it a good occasion for getting drunk. But he answers Macduff's joke about it quite aptly, and his delay in opening the gates can presumably be accounted for by his unwilling waking, the getting on of clothes and boots, and the finding a light for his lantern. Drunk on this occasion and on others he may have been, but it does not prove him a confirmed sot.

Banquo's murderers are commonly made ruffians fetched from the gutter. But the text's implication is surely that they were officers, cast perhaps for some misdemeanour and out of luck. Certainly the lovely lines,

> The west yet glimmers with some streaks of day.
> Now spurs the lated traveller apace
> To gain the timely inn,

are not gutter-bred, and Macbeth's speech to them, beginning,

> Ay, in the catalogue ye go for men,

loses half its point if they are not men come down in the world. The third murderer is obviously a private and particular spy of Macbeth's, and his unheralded appearance (like that of the fellow who warns Lady Macduff of her danger) is in itself significant enough, significant too of the whole state of Macbeth's kingdom, with its spies, and spies upon spies; when, as Rosse says,

> . . . we hold rumour
> From what we fear, yet know not what we fear.

We must note, too, the masterly effect produced when these three stand with Banquo's body at their feet, the light out, and the stillness around—which they but half break with their curt whispering.

It is important that the doctor and the waiting gentlewoman should not—as the stage phrase goes—try to play Lady Macbeth's part for her in the sleep-walking scene. He is intent on his case, she mainly obsessed with a queen's waiting-woman's anxiety to hush up the scandal. Beside Lady Macbeth herself they must seem pettifogging, or she cannot show tragic to the full. The doctor has his couplet too, when Macbeth has flung off the stage in berserk rage:

> Were I from Dunsinane away and clear,
> Profit again should hardly draw me here.

This has been condemned as un-Shakespearean and beneath the dignity of the tragedy. But when Shakespeare saw a chance to salt the meat of his plays with such touches he did not stand upon tragic dignity. He had enough of that to spare and to waste upon us whenever he chose.

Duncan can hardly be misread. He is often made older than need be, and sometimes too consistently meek and usually too lachrymose. There are actors with an unhappy knack of taking one point in a part—and a minor one—as a peg upon which to hang the whole. And Duncan's 'plenteous joys' seeking to hide themselves in 'drops of sorrow' are apt to be used to water the character down to an undue depression; and with this will sag the play's whole beginning, one aspect of which the king's figure must dominate. His arrival at Inverness should be, in a simple way, as stately as possible. His lines here have fine turns of thought and feeling, and a most royal ring about them. And

> By your leave, hostess,

seems to indicate that, as the custom was, he kisses Lady Macbeth's cheek. What better climax and ending could the scene have?

The problem of presenting the weird sisters is more deeply rooted than in any corruption of the text. We can cut away most of Middleton with confidence, and quite banish his creatures of comic opera from our minds, and the remainder may be true Shakespeare; but what the positive embodiment of Shakespeare's conception should be this simple sum in subtraction by no means leaves clear. That he himself calls them weird sisters and not (provably) witches is something, and might lead us straight to Holinshed's 'three women in strange and wild apparel, resembling creatures of elder world', if it were not that both Holinshed in another passage and Shakespeare's own writing of the later scene give equal colour to a more commonplace conception. This part of Act IV, Scene i, is intrinsically more Shakespearean than the earlier scenes in which the witches appear without Macbeth—though, truly, it is a weakness in criticism to be always maintaining that what is well done is by Shakespeare and what is ill done is by somebody else. This, however, is the more likely to be Shakespeare in that Holinshed's creatures for this particular purpose are 'certaine wizards' and 'a certaine witch'.[24] Yet Macbeth says that he will to the 'weird sisters'. It seems pretty clear that Shakespeare deliberately blended the two types. In the composite as we have it there is risk in claiming too much emphasis for the first. He may have continued to call them the weird sisters only because he had begun by calling them so. On the other hand, the part of their witchcraft that is essential to the play is given dignity and mystery, and it may be—it *may* be—that their incantations round the cauldron, which are given strength and good colour but no more, are, in form at least, Middleton's after all.

When it comes to their presentation on the stage one may perhaps proceed usefully by negation. Though they have supernatural powers, they are *not* supernatural beings. They are *not*, on the other hand, the sort of old women that Shakespeare may have seen ducked in the horse-pond at Stratford. And if his superstitious fancies on those occasions glorified such poor wretches somewhat, we should still be bound for stage purposes to consider a little what our fancies would confer on the same figures.

If we look, where we should usually look for a description, to the impression made upon some opposite character, to whom it is given to interpret an unusual figure to the audience, we find:

> ... What are these
> So wither'd and so wild in their attire,
> That look not like th' inhabitants o' the earth
> And yet are on't?

and again:

> How now, you secret, black, and midnight hags!

And that surely paints them for us with sufficient clarity.

The last part of the play calls for the producer's very firm control of the elements that may otherwise, so to speak, run away with it. It is notable—though in the play's staging as a rule too little noticed—with what a very strong hand Shakespeare himself has controlled them. One need not again inveigh against the senseless omission from most productions of such a scene as that in which the revolted Scottish lords gather together, nor against the telescoping of those that picture Malcolm's advance. This misconduct alone tends to pile up the other part of the action into a lurid chaos and to make the strain on any player of Macbeth unbearable. But, right to the end, Shakespeare has most carefully balanced the horrible by the heroic. Young Siward's death and his father's fortitude is set against Macbeth's slaughtering and the uplifting of his severed head. And to wallow in the horror and omit the beauty and dignity is to degrade great tragedy to the depth of poor melodrama.

In character development Shakespeare has perhaps done all he can do—for his protagonists at least—even before the end of Act III. The rest is catastrophe, skilfully retarded. But in his marshalling of the play's action to its end, he surely outdoes even his own accustomed mastery in such matters. We have, in the scene with the weird sisters, the whipping up of the evil in Macbeth to the top of its fury, immediately followed by its most

savage outbreak—sudden and short—upon Lady Macduff and the child. Then comes, as we have remarked,
the elaborate and weighty preparation for the play's
counter-action; an outspoken scene. In contrast to this
follows the scene of sickness and whisperings and unnatural troubles, the scene of the slow perishing of one
of the two evil beings of the play. Quickly after comes
the gathering of the Scottish lords, like men escaping
from prison and despair. The 'drum and colours' here
strike a new note; lifted spirits are marked by such means
as the rising inflection of Angus's second speech with its
'Now ... Now ... Now ...'; and the repeated 'March
we on' and 'Make we our march' begins the movement
to the play's end.

Macbeth himself is, so to say, the fixed point towards
which this movement sweeps. We are to see him at
intervals, waiting the approach and desperate at having
to wait, for this, as we know, was not his sort of
soldiership. In the first of these scenes of his we have
talk of preparation, but Shakespeare allows it none of
the cheerful panoply of war, neither 'drum' nor 'colours'.
Instead there is depression and distraction, the news of
the flying of the Thanes, the terror of the 'cream-faced
loon', and, to clinch the effect, Macbeth's own contrari-
ness about his armour—one of those simple touches that
help to throw great issues into relief.

The following scene is so short that it is possible to
give it the effect of an unhalting march. The Scottish
and English armies are joined, their number is doubled.
Malcolm has the leadership. But the last two voices are
Macduff's and Siward's—to whom a very ringing speech
is given, emphasis of his dignity and importance as the
English general.

Now on Macbeth's side the martial note is sounded,
and sounded loudly. This scene is more rhythmically

written than his earlier one, and is meant to be more rapid. It has but two checks to its pace, the news of the Queen's death, and the couplet,

> I' gin to be aweary of the sun;

and the latter may be designed to emphasize by contrast the rush of the end. The bringing of the news of the moving wood immediately upon the first reflective moment indicates an even greater contrast. At this point, if one were charting the scene as a fever is charted, one would show a perpendicular leap in energy. And the mere vocal effect of the passage beginning,

> Arm, arm, and out,

should be in itself an alarum bell.

Then follows, again, an interesting check and contrast. Malcolm's army is before Dunsinane, at rest for a moment. He and Siward coolly plan their battle. The trumpet-toned couplet at the end is given, for obvious reasons, to Macduff.

The actual conduct of the last scene upon Shakespeare's stage we have already discussed. Its inward scheme is not hard to determine, though, with so much movement involved, it may not be too easy to abide by in practice. It divides, dramatically, into three parts. The first runs to Macduff's discovery of Macbeth with

> Turn, hell-hound, turn.

This goes, as we say, ding-dong, and any possible half-pauses are filled up with 'alarums'. Macbeth is grim and deadly, a trapped beast; his comings and goings have no purpose in them. Moreover, as the battle goes forward he becomes conscious that his mind too has been trapped and tricked, though he cannot yet see how. He is invulnerable; again and again he returns to this. But, as certainly, with the battle against him, he is doomed. Is the answer to the riddle that he must kill himself? Must he 'play the Roman fool'? He fights, one would suppose, like an automaton and perhaps the more dangerously for that.

In clear contrast is the gallant, crusading figure of young Siward, flashing to his death.

There is none of the glow of battle upon Macduff. Methodically, determinedly, he pursues his single purpose. For a relief we have the interlude when the two generals, cool and confident still, enter the castle.

The second part concerns Macbeth and Macduff alone. Nice critics have found Macbeth's last fling of words—beloved of every schoolboy—too highly flavoured with bombast. They may be. But Shakespeare, having brought his play to the issue of sheer physical combat, might well think it appropriate to throw niceness behind him.[25] This is to be a mortal combat and a mighty combat. For Macduff to come easily by his vengeance would be unsatisfying. For Macbeth to go easily out would be incredible, and to give him a finely worded end might seem to redeem him, if ever so little. This Shakespeare will not do. He allows him one gleam of incorrigible pride, he leaves him his animal courage. For the rest, he sends him shouting to hell. And from the beginning the exchange of speeches between the two men should be like the exchange of blows.

The end of the play is contrived as a full and varied orchestra of voices with the trumpets of victory topping them. Malcolm and his soldiers enter processionally, and at once we are given the suggestion of order restored. The note of pity for the dead is struck, and upon it comes the practised soldier's stoic response. There is Rosse's smooth sympathy. There is the defiant nobility with which Siward takes his own son's death;

and for Malcolm there is a needed touch of impulsive generosity.

Macduff's entrance, lifting the severed head, changes the key almost violently. Here is an echo of the now ended tragedy. Vengeance is accomplished, but Macduff, widowed and childless, stands apart from all thoughtless rejoicing.

> I see thee compassed with thy kingdom's pearl.

But he is a man alone. His voice must have the music of a selfless and unforgettable sorrow in it.

Then, with the careful modulation of Malcolm's address to his people, Shakespeare brings us at his ease back to our work-a-day world.

Notes

1 Incidentally it must be noted that in the text they are never referred to as witches, but always as the Weird Sisters. For witches the stage directions in the Folio are alone responsible. To these—with a text so extensively corrupted—it is difficult to assign consistent value. Where they pertain to the corrupted parts the balance of probability is that they are never Shakespearean. Otherwise they may be good evidence of the traditional staging of the play, but that will be the limit of their authority. The intrinsic evidence upon this question I deal with later.

2 The difficulty about the Thane of Cawdor can indeed be overcome by assuming that Macbeth is not 'Bellona's bridegroom'. Why must we suppose he is? For one thing, if the same battle is referred to, there would be little dramatic point in Duncan's question to Rosse,

> Whence cam'st thou, worthy thane?

and the answer

> From Fife, great king.

Certainly the duplication of 'Norweyan' is confusing. But are
not these the facts? 'The merciless Macdonwald', joined with
a 'Norweyan lord,' was beaten by Macbeth and Banquo.
Norway himself and the Thane of Cawdor were beaten by
some other general. Even so it is strange that Angus should
say questioningly of Cawdor,

> ... Whether he was combin'd
> With those of Norway, or did line the rebel
> With hidden help and vantage, or that with both
> He labour'd in his country's wrack, I know not.

Shakespeare was not apt to leave things in such a muddle at
the beginning of a play.

And all this does not, of course, exhaust the difficulties of
the first four scenes as they appear in the Folio. The Mac-
beth-Duncan meeting is unsatisfactory. Moreover—and more
importantly—the disclosure of Macbeth's mind, not in a
soliloquy, but in two rather ineptly contrived asides, is surely,
in such a play and with such a character, un-Shakespearean.

Even if—as some critics suppose—the explanation was that
he hurriedly compressed an elaborately planned opening in
order to arrive more swiftly at Duncan's murder, we should
still expect to find the work more skilfully done. Here is a
fantastic guess; but it might really be that when it came to
printing the Folio the manuscript of the first four scenes—of
Middleton's revision even—had vanished, and that what we
have is the result of the mobilising of memories of actors and
prompter. Some lines they recalled accurately, some they
confused, and some they had forgotten altogether.

3 Macbeth must have time to get on his nightgown and wash
his hands.

4 They show distinct signs of being an interpolation, but it
does not follow they are Middleton's. Shakespeare himself
might have found good reason for lengthening the scene in
a wish to give greater importance to the two characters. See
infra.

5 It cannot remain to the play's end. What is to hide it from
Malcolm and Siward?

6 This would involve a momentarily empty stage, but the pause would be filled by alarums. It is a question, of course, how easily accessible the gallery at the Globe was from the lower stage.

7 Or the dialogue to the fight might even be spoken from the lower to the upper stage.

8 But for the actor's treatment of this, see infra.

9 Though, actually, no swifter movement is well possible than that for which the Elizabethan stage provides.

10 One need not spend time contending it was Shakespeare's. For is Shakespeare's discoverable? Upon what basis of dramatic advantage or practical convenience was it founded?

11 The scene is most important, and has only come to be thought otherwise by the insistent viewing of the play as a dramatic preserve for the performances of Macbeth and Lady Macbeth.

12 An Elizabethan nightgown, needless to say, was more a dressing-gown than a garment to sleep in.

13 The illustrator of the original volume.

14 I do not know whether any archaeologically minded producer has yet substituted bagpipes.

15 If he can be thought of as breaking suddenly away from the jovial company, unable to play his hypocritical part in it any longer, a much needed impetus is given to the soliloquy.

16 Incidentally the play's balance will probably at once be upset, for no actor of good instinct will allow a performance to hang fire, and if the Lady Macbeth will not set a pace the Macbeth will be tempted to, much to the prejudice of his own character's development.

17 Shakespeare hardly ever marks down the physical appearance of his characters. In Falstaff, of course, he does. But, in a sense, Falstaff's bulk *is* his character. Maria in *Twelfth Night* is 'the youngest wren of nine'. But the repeated insistence upon her diminutiveness seems to denote a particular player.

18 By nothing I say do I mean to imply that such a thing as the acting of fragility is impossible. But Mrs Siddons—for an instance—apparently found herself at too great a physical disadvantage in the matter, and abandoned all attempt to suggest it.

19 Macbeth's views upon blood-guiltiness, however, were somewhat narrow, if our interpretation of

> Thou canst not say I did it

may hold. He would then expect his wife to be whole-heartedly glad, for his sake, that Banquo was out of the way; it was enough for him to keep her in a most formal sense innocent of the knowledge for her to be able to applaud the deed with a clear conscience.

20 To read

> But in them nature's copy's not eterne

as a suggestion of murder is quite wrong. From the point of view of the play's action a temptation to do what is already in the doing is weak. And this one line must then obscure the obvious meaning of every other line Lady Macbeth speaks in the scene.

21 For the foundations of Macbeth's character, and especially for a study of that power of conscienceless imagination that dominates it, one cannot do better than turn to the masterly *Shakespearean Tragedy* of A. C. Bradley.

22 May I register an opinion, though, that it is *Malcolm's* eye in Scotland that would create soldiers, and that it is Macbeth who is referred to as having no children. There is no proving this. But the implication that Macduff is there turning to Rosse for comfort is an unnatural one.

23 He is silent at the discovery of Duncan's murder, and modern editions even omit to mark his entrance, which F1 gives with Macbeth and Lenox; but his silent presence can be made most effective. Or is the direction evidence of a mere stage-manager's anxiety to augment his crowd, and did Shakespeare's Rosse think it more politic to stay in bed when he heard the alarm bell?

24 True, Shakespeare might have disregarded Holinshed here and Middleton, by a coincidence, have adhered to him. By coincidence, because he would hardly have deliberately rejected Shakespeare and yet sought Shakespeare's source.

25 Not that he ever took much stock in it.

<u>Notes</u>